PRAISE
ULTI

"Steve and Sally have written a powerful book that bridges Jesus' teachings and healings with ancient shamanic healing practice demonstrating that Jesus had great knowledge and training in the techniques of shamanism. This much needed book is a wealth of information and offers much to people of all traditions who have an interest in healing."

—Jose Luis Stevens Ph.D., author of *How To Pray The Shaman's Way* and *Awaken the Inner Shaman.*

"If you have worried that shamanism is inconsistent with your Christian faith, or if you've been told that shamanism is a demonic practice in opposition to true faith, this book is an important read for you. The authors offer multiple examples of shamanic practice found throughout Christian scriptures and the life of Jesus. They make a clear case that shamanism is not a faith in itself, but a set of practices that help you work with the Creator to bring healing and deeper awareness into life."

—Jaime Meyer, President, Society for Shamanic Practice; M.A., Theology and The Arts.

"This volume is written in the vane of Drs. Michael S. Heiser, Ph.D. and Bradford Keeney, Ph.D. It offers readers an inspiring portal to fresh understanding of the interconnectedness of all creation. For the practicing Christian it opens the door to a wider vision of the 'unseen' and for so many the 'unused' power that is available to all who will open their hearts, minds and spirit."

—Murray Flagg, PhD. Murray holds degrees in Business, Theology and Communication and has been a pastor, denominational leader, university instructor and a consultant to major corporations. Having lived and worked in The U.S., the South Pacific and Europe, Murray is now an ordained Christian Clergy minister as well as Shamanic Practitioner.

"Steve and Sally challenge the limits of our preconceived understandings about what the Spirit can do in and through us. This book makes us think. It challenges us to see the actions of Jesus and the Holy Spirit in ways we haven't imagined. Whether or not we agree with what Steve and Sally present, we are made to wonder what God might be doing through us for the healing of the world."

—Rev. Jean Hurst, M. Div., Presbyterian Pastor

"Jesus' miraculous power invites readers of the bible to wonder if they can be brought into the present. Steve and Sally share their personal exploration of his healings as incredible shamanic works with solid biblical support. Christians exploring spiritual and shamanic healing practices conflicted with their own faith may find this illuminating and very helpful."

—Alan Davis, MD PhD

"Steve and Sally offer a fresh perspective on the connection between your spiritual life and shamanic practices, sharing ways to enhance your faith on many levels."

—Lois Melkonian, PCC, Fellow Coach at BetterUp, Writer/ Podcaster focusing on strategic shifts, influence, identity and purpose and meaning."

JESUS, THE ULTIMATE SHAMAN

Enriching Life through Shamanic Practices

STEPHEN M. BULL
SALLY H. DENNY

APOCRYPHILE
PRESS

Apocryphile Press
1100 County Route 54
Hannacroix, NY 12087
www.apocryphilepress.com

Copyright © 2022 by Stephen M. Bull & Sally H. Denny
ISBN 978-1-955821-78-0 | paper
ISBN 978-1-955821-79-7 | ePub
Printed in the United States of America

Cover image © "The Apache Christ" by Robert Lentz, courtesy of Trinity
Stores, www.trinitystores.com, 800.699.4482

Please join our mailing list at www.apocryphilepress.com/free. We'll keep you
up-to-date on all our new releases, and we'll also send you a FREE BOOK. Visit
us today!

CONTENTS

ACKNOWLEDGMENTS

This book has been a good and long project, including many hours of discussion with friends about how to present the contents of this book. Before acknowledging the powerful and insightful help our friends have provided, we'd like you to know that we have "test-driven" all of the practices taught here resulting in the healing of many people from their physical, spiritual, and emotional anomalies. The point is, we practice what we preach! We have not done this work alone but through the power of the (Holy) Spirit[1] and with the aid of our helping spirits.

Don and Alison Daley not only encouraged us to write this book but were always ready with their friendship at necessary times to combat our frustrations. Don and Ali are deeply insightful people who have a great amount of experience working in the spirit realm and on whom we rely for advice when it comes to matters of the Spirit. Don and Ali produced the wonderful piece on drumming in the Shamanic Tools chapter and the dream content in the Spiritual Gifts chapter. As Don said, "When you get that book written . . . ," and so we did. Furthermore, we give them credit for helping to create part of the title to this book.

We asked several conservative Christian friends, Vern Van Buskirk and Jim Black, for feedback. They run closer to the literacy of the Bible than we do. We appreciate their feedback, their reading of the manuscript, and their thoughtful suggestions and challenges. Their input, though many times in conflict with our ideas, helped clarify and sharpen our thinking.

We give a special thanks to our Shaman mentors, Kenny Emerson and José Luis Stephens, Ph.D.

Not only have we taken several shamanic classes from Kenny, but we've talked with Kenny and his wife, Carol, about ways in which Christian living and Shamanism fit together.

We were touched that Dr. Stevens would take the time to read our entire book and offer constructive criticisms. It was Dr. Stevens who led us to obtain the much-needed services of a writing coach, which led to a significant revision of the book. It is Dr. Stevens who graciously agreed to write the Foreword to our book. And of course, we must mention the powerful learning that has come to us through The Power Path, directed by Dr. Stevens, his wife Lena, and their daughter Anna. Our sincerest thanks.

Kim O'Hara, our writing coach and friend, took a dusty, somewhat boring scholarly document and helped us reformat and repackage it so that it is more conversational and much easier to read and understand. We are grateful for her expertise and belief in us. Ms. O'Hara is a very insightful woman. Her business, *A Story Inside*, and her proficiency in helping writers shape how their books are drafted, is well worth any author's attention.

We also thank several of our friends who took the time to read through our document and offer helpful feedback. You know who you are and we are very grateful for your help and suggestions for improvements.

ABBREVIATIONS

All Scripture verses are from the New King James version[1] unless otherwise noted. Old and New Testament chapters and their abbreviations follow.

OLD TESTAMENT

Genesis / Gen.
Exodus / Ex.
Numbers / Nu.
Deuteronomy / Dt.
Leviticus / Lev.
Judges / Jud.
Joshua / Jos.
1 Samuel / 1 Sam.
2 Kings / 2 Kgs.
2 Chronicles / 2 Chron.
Nehemiah / Neh.
Psalms / Ps.
Proverbs / Prov.
Isaiah / Is.

Jeremiah / Jer.
Ezekiel / Ezek.
Daniel / Dan.
Amos / Amos
Zechariah / Zech.

NEW TESTAMENT

Matthew / Mt.
Mark / Mk.
Luke / Lk.
John / Jn.
Acts / Acts
Romans / Rom.
1 Corinthians / 1 Cor.
2 Corinthians / 2 Cor.
Ephesians / Eph.
Philippians / Phil.
Colossians / Col.
1 Thessalonians / 1 These.
1 Timothy / 1 Tim.
2 Timothy / 2 Tim.
Titus / Titus
Hebrews / Heb.
1 Peter / 1 Pet.
2 Peter / 2 Pet.
Jude / Jude
Revelation / Rev.

FOREWORD

BY JOSÉ LUIS STEVENS, PH.D.

In this powerful book about Shamanism, Sally Denny and Steve Bull boldly and perceptively draw the parallels between the role and work of a Shaman and the position Jesus occupied in his ministry and in his community. In the course of his life Jesus played many roles and was identified with many activities.

For a Christian, Jesus was the Son of God. It is fair to say, however, he was also a good student, a powerful teacher, a family member, a citizen, a carpenter, a healer, and a preacher. Some would even say he was a revolutionary, a politician, a doctor, and a social change agent. He has also been compared with CEOs and superstars. Is it such a stretch to say he was also a highly competent Shaman?

To be a Shaman was and still is a leadership position involving officiating at ceremonies, gathering knowledge, teaching, storytelling, public speaking, making tribal decisions, creating art, and protecting the community. As Steve and Sally accurately portray, Shamans were the elders of their communities, the teachers, the healers, the earliest doctors and psychologists. As we have just seen, Jesus was all of these things and more.

In fact, what I love about Steve and Sally's approach in this book is that they humanize Jesus, make him more accessible, help us to understand that he was very much a human being who learned skills and used tools like everyone else in his time. He ate food like everyone, needed to sleep and rest, and worked hard when he saw the need. And like everyone he learned to use the tools of his trades.

People often don't stop to consider that Jesus, having a human body with opposable thumbs, was an excellent tool user. Undoubtedly as a carpenter's son he learned to use a saw and a hammer because those are some of the tools of that trade. Clearly, he used many tools during the course of his life, like all people do—a cup or chalice for drinking, sandals to walk in, a blanket for sleeping and so on. These are all various types of tools that a person needs on a daily basis just to get by. So, with this in mind it is not hard to understand that he used shamanic tools as well to perform the great numbers of healings that he engaged in.

It is well understood that Shamanism is an age-old collection of techniques and skills that allow a person to diagnose and perform healings for various maladies and illnesses. Interestingly, these healing techniques were known and used by Shamans on all continents over long stretches of time even though they had little contact with one another. When we read about various healings that Jesus performed it becomes evident that he knew and used basic shamanic skills in carrying out these healings just as he knew how to do many other things in his life. The laying on of hands is a classic shamanic skill, as is casting out demons and sending an illness into the flames of a fire—they are classical techniques of Shamans everywhere.

On my many travels to study with Shamans and to study the knowledge of Shamanism, I have run into Shamans who, in addition to their shamanic practice, were also devout followers in a great variety of religions—Tibetan Buddhism, Hinduism,

Catholicism, Taoism, Evangelical Christianity, Huna, Native American spirituality, Incan, Mayan, Toltec, and yes, even Islam. Clearly then, Shamanism is more a way of doing things than a religion since it has no book, no hierarchy or leader, and no dogma. In this respect many people have been mistaken as to the true nature of Shamanism. It is more like saying someone is a pragmatist rather than saying they are a Hindu. And yet Shamans are definitely involved in spiritual practice. They honor the web of life, the interconnectedness of all things, and they see Spirit in everything and everyone. They address Spirit in all their ceremonies and they pray frequently. They employ spiritual allies to help them in situations too difficult to figure out under ordinary means.

Most Shamans performing service in their local communities never become famous or well-known outside of their communities and as a consequence we do not hear or learn about Shamanism in everyday life. However, Jesus became very well-known historically, not because he sought fame but simply because of who he was and the power of his expression. Therefore, he is a powerful and wonderful example of a Shaman that we can witness practicing his trade to perfection.

I like that Steve and Sally have been able to connect examples from quantum physics to Jesus' ministry because in Shamanism we can see many examples of quantum physics at work. In Toltec Shamanism for example, there is a concept that for something such as an illness to exist, it has to have a container made up of particles. They say you cannot remove the illness without removing the container that holds it in physical form. In other words, they found a way to describe disappearing something unwanted in terms that are now understood by physicists. As evidenced by his healing techniques Jesus was well aware of the practice of disappearing disease. He knew how to issue psychic commands that take apart the particles that hold something together and release them so that his patient no longer suffered from the malady. He knew that matter responds to thought and observation, just as the physicists say it does. With a thought, he could heal—and this is the heart of shamanic practice, using thought and intention to reorganize matter. As Jesus predicted, someday this will eventually be a widespread practice.

The authors do a thorough job verifying through Scripture that healers accessing universal knowledge and working with many spirits are sincerely doing God's work when they heal injury, disease, and psychological problems whether or not they identify as Christian. They further reveal through Psalms that objects of nature like the sun, the animals, the trees, and the sea are all considered to be conscious and know who their Creator is. Not only is the biblical position that they are conscious, but that they help and assist human beings as helping spirits. This is exactly the Shaman's understanding of the physical reality we live in.

The authors also lay out in a very organized way through Scripture the reason that shamanic practice is aligned with Christian ways. For example, they delve into the issue of authorization: where Shamans derive their authority and where Christians should derive theirs—the cosmic Christ embedded in Jesus' teachings. They explain the importance of melding the heart with the head, combining reason with the heart's knowledge, and show how important this is to Christians and Shamans both. It is the essence of their understanding of the cosmos.

They take a deep dive into the whole issue of divination, mediumship, and prophecy and explain how many Christians have been led to believe that these abilities damn Shamanism from the Christian perspective and how these prejudices don't add up to a true understanding of either Shamanism or Christianity.

Referencing Einstein's explanations of the nature of time, they thoughtfully dispose of any notions that the shamanic practice of future telling is the same as mere fortune telling, nor is it occult or wrong-minded, but rather a product of natural laws.

In Part Two Sally and Steve shift to practical methods to open up to and actualize practices and tools of shamanic healing and how to protect oneself from any harm while utilizing these abilities. This is the part that becomes quite interesting, as they move from the discussion of what shamanism is to the actual practice of healing, clearing, and promoting health. In the end they make a strong case for shamanic practice enhancing and strengthening a person's path whatever their faith perspective.

They explain the role of intuition and make clear that one need not choose rationalism over spiritualism or vice versa but that both can work together quite nicely. In fact, balancing them is quite necessary for overall health and vitality. In addition, they make a powerful argument for developing the art of listening, for developing self-confidence, and for increasing your ability to trust what you perceive—as opposed to what others have told you to perceive—as ways of developing your shamanic healing skills. From the practice of meditation to the shamanic journey method, the use of allies and helpers to the use of sound through drumming and rattling to shift your perception, Steve and Sally take you through a variety of traditional shamanic tools to enhance your skills and get you started on a path dedicated to healing and supporting those in need. They discuss extractions, retrieval of lost aspects of the self, and a whole host of more advanced shamanic techniques to introduce the reader to the vast possibilities of this complex yet straightforward set of practices.

In the end the authors emphasize that it is Jesus' ministry that teaches a great deal about the methods of Shamans and the healing path. Jesus taught extensively about the importance of Spirit, dreams, and visions. With many examples of their experience healing people's illnesses in everyday life, they bring shamanic practice into concrete and practical clarity. Kudos to

Sally and Steve for their visionary and brave book introducing the age-old interface between shamanic practice and the Christian way of life.

José Luis Stevens, Ph.D. is the author of How to Pray the Shaman's Way: Ancient Techniques For Extraordinary Results.

PART I
STEPPING INTO A NEW AND DIFFERENT
REALITY

I magine you are out for a walk along the shore of the ocean or a large lake. You are in awe of what you see and say to yourself, "It's all here—the trees, the rocks, the sand, the water, the wildlife." But we would ask you, "Is it 'all' really here? Is 'everything' contained in what you see?"

The answer is "No," because all you have to do is don a face-mask, snorkel, and fins, submerge beneath the water, and you come face-to-face with a whole new and different underwater reality. If you dove into the ocean, you might be dazzled by countless sea stars and anemones; long, graceful strands of waving seaweed; crowds of beautiful, multi-colored fish. It's the kind of experience where, when you come out of the water, you can't stop talking about it!

This is exactly what happened when we were introduced to Shamanism. We thought our previous reality was the only one to experience, but we were wrong. Just beyond the surface, so to speak, we encountered a spirit realm that is vast and powerful and helpful. And of course, we couldn't stop talking about it! We are here to introduce you to that world.

In Part One, we will help you:

- Build a foundation for an informed understanding of Shamanism.
- View the shamanic practices of Jesus that you may never have considered when reading the Bible.
- Learn where Shamans draw their wisdom from, and explain why it is not a questionable source—quite the contrary!
- Understand about the existence of helping spirits who do the work of the Spirit and who help us.
- Realize that Shamanism and the Christ-life are complementary and not competitive.
- See that Jesus expected His followers not to get bogged down in the chapter-and-verse of the Bible and miss the spiritual realities it reveals.
- Discover that shamanic "divination" has everything to do with healing and nothing to do with fortune-telling or demonism.

So welcome to a new world, a shamanic world that we've been exploring for some years now. Set your fears aside, your preconceived ideas and judgments, and let this new reality come to you, embrace you, speak to you. From us to you, many blessings in your new adventure. And enjoy!

SHAMANISM AND CHRISTIAN PRACTICE

P eople develop naturally as Creator made them to do, but that growth can be hindered when they are wounded or traumatized. What are the ingredients of healing that make it possible for people to change and come out from under their woundedness or trauma and be made whole? How does healing happen on a deeper, spirit-soul basis? These are the questions we are focusing on in this book.

Healing is our passion and possibly yours. The greatest healer, of course, was Jesus. Have you considered how Jesus healed? He healed not only in word but in deed. One of the "deeds" we discover about Jesus is that He seemed to use shamanic practices to heal throughout His ministry. Does it surprise you that Jesus used shamanic practices? This may seem like a foreign concept to you, but we want to show you how it's true. You may be surprised to learn how Shamanism not only played a part in Jesus' ministry but can contribute to your knowledge of healing as well.

Have you maintained the belief that only God can heal? Your thinking may follow this line of reasoning: Since we are not God, we cannot heal others; only God can heal. You may remember, however, that Jesus gave His disciples power to heal (Lk. 9. 1).

He told His followers in the last chapter of Mark's gospel that one of the signs that would follow them was their ability to heal.

You might wonder, "What does Jesus have to do with Shamanism?" A fact you may not know and that we want to share with you is that much of what Jesus did in His ministry was done by Shamans throughout the world prior to His life and even afterwards to the present day. We want to clearly state, however, that our declaring that Jesus used shamanic tools does not in any way demote Him from being Deity, the Son of God.

Consider that Jesus did not operate outside of His culture or even outside the practices that circulated through the Middle East where He lived. He relied on and used shamanic practices that were common to His era and culture.

When you think about it, Jesus had many "options" for how to conduct his ministry. For instance, Jesus did not need to do remote healings, but He did them. Nor did He need to spend time alone, on a mountain, in deep meditation, but He did. He did not have to go away and fast and pray in the wilderness for forty days and nights. Many of the things Jesus did are consistent with shamanic practices found throughout the world. These practices offer us, as practitioners, incredible power, especially the power to heal—if we use them!

Now when we talk to people about their concept of Jesus, they use various words to describe Him: healer, priest, counselor, exorcist, even political activist. But if you mention that He was a "Shaman," eyebrows are raised or there is a slight cough as if to say, "Oh no. Shamans are strange and bad. Jesus couldn't have operated shamanically." Well, we believe he did. But first, let's begin our education and learn more about Shamanism.

A BRIEF LOOK INTO SHAMANISM

Did you know that the practice of Shamanism dates back thousands of years—certainly forty thousand years, but possibly as long as seventy-five thousand years ago? And it is also noteworthy that Shamanism has been practiced on every continent, across many diverse cultures throughout the world over thousands of years. It is still being practiced today. There is an amazing consistency of beliefs and practices across all cultures despite there being no contact between Shamans within the various people groups.[1]

These facts about Shamanism made a tremendous impact on our thinking. First, we realized that Shamanism is not a religion; rather, it is a set of universal skills derived from universal knowledge that is available to all people down through time. Shamans tap into this universal field of knowledge. Even Jesus, who walked the Earth not only as God but as man, used universal knowledge as well.

UNIVERSAL KNOWLEDGE AND JESUS KNOWLEDGE

"Universal knowledge" is the same kind of knowledge that is studied by biologists, chemists, physicists, cosmologists, medical doctors, etc. It is knowledge that pertains to the laws, principles, and properties that govern our world. Shamans access and work with universal knowledge, but it is available to anyone who seeks it.

In addition to universal knowledge, there also is a body of knowledge that comes from the Bible that relates specifically to who Jesus was (His identity, whom He claimed to be) and His mission (why the Christ incarnated in Jesus and lived on earth as a man). Let's call this "Jesus knowledge," or scriptural revelation.

Many Christians may believe that Shamans must accept "Jesus knowledge," or else their universal shamanic knowledge and skills are invalid. This is inaccurate. It is our belief that a person can practice shamanic skills (use universal knowledge) whether they believe in "Jesus knowledge" or not.

For instance, if a person does not believe in Jesus, their lack of belief in "Jesus truth" does not negate whatever universal truths they use. For example, it doesn't negate the universal law of gravity. Universal truth stands on its own merit no matter what a person's religious or spiritual beliefs are. Universal truth is truth and does not change based on one's opinion or faith perspective.

Think of it this way. You probably use the services of an attorney, a medical doctor, or a dentist without inquiring about their private faith, right? That's because you are more interested in the practitioner's skill—what they know as "universal knowledge." It is no different regarding Shamans. We do not have to be concerned about the private faith of a Shaman, because it is the universal knowledge they possess and the skill they derive therefrom that make them effective healers. In other words— news flash!—Shamans can work with Christians to expand their skills without causing Christians to deny their faith.

We see this in the ministry of Jesus. That is, the universal knowledge—the shamanic skills—Jesus used existed side-by-side with the "Jesus knowledge" He taught about Himself. Just as Jesus incorporated both types of knowledge in His life and ministry, we can do the same. That is, the universal shamanic practices of Jesus can provide helpful guidance for healers, but we can also pay attention to the "Jesus knowledge" that scripture reveals. Our hope is that you find this opportunity to learn about shamanic skills as exciting as we do and that you will allow it to expand your understanding and grant you access to more powerful tools to do your healing work.

THE HEALING BENEFIT FROM LEARNING SHAMANIC SKILLS

So, you might ask, "What is the benefit to Christians of learning shamanic methods?" The answer is that shamanic processes provide Christians with powerful ways to heal. In fact, shamanic tools can enrich everyone's life, no matter their belief system, enabling them to heal.

We never know when a situation will arise that will require us to utilize various shamanic tools we've learned in order to bring healing to someone or to relieve them from physical pain. In one instance, Steve was meeting with a physical therapist who was wearing a foot boot. He asked if she was in pain. When she said yes and explained the injury, Steve asked if he might help relieve her pain. She sat down and set her foot up on his leg, boot and all, where he was able to move energy in order to promote her healing and relieve her discomfort. As Jesus healed spontaneously and out of compassion, we should be ready and available to do the same. Shamanism gives us specific tools enabling us to do that.

OTHER BENEFITS

Shamanism can also assist us in developing our spiritual senses and give us a way to apply our spiritual gifts in a more focused, effective way. It can instruct us how to access not only the Holy Spirit but "helping spirits" that are before the throne of God and who can contribute significantly to the healing process.[2]

WHAT LED US TO BEGIN THE USE OF SHAMANIC PRACTICES

Each of us has a story about how we have progressed through life in relation to the growth of our faith. Someday, hopefully, we will meet some of you (through our website, http://www.transforming-lives.us) and learn what sparked your interest in Shamanism. But for now, here's how we arrived at this place.

STEVE

I was raised Roman Catholic. In my twenties I became what is termed a "born again Christian," that is, I made the choice to follow Christ for myself and not because I grew up in a Church. I was surfing with a fellow who challenged me to read the Bible. I accepted the "challenge" and became instantly enamored with Jesus, His simplicity, His truthfulness, and His power.

I was attending law school at that time. I had an experience that forever changed my life. I was surfing, waiting for waves, when a voice spoke to me (whom I now know to be the Spirit—my first experience). It stated matter-of-factly, "You're going to seminary." "Ha," I shouted, "no way." I literally threw my surfboard into my van and drove home. The voice returned day after day while driving to law school until, finally, I gave in. It was the first major call of the Spirit in my life.

I enrolled at Fuller Theological Seminary in SoCal, acquired a Master of Divinity degree, and worked as a mountaineering guide for a faith-based outdoor education program. Next, I lay-pastored a Young Marrieds' Group in Seal Beach, CA. The church I attended stated their belief in the Holy Spirit, but Spirit seemed more of a theory to them than an actual practice. During that time, however, I began to speak in tongues. This did not occur at a church service or conference. It happened when I was alone during a season of intense, intercessory prayer. Bang! Another experience with Spirit, ever shaping, ever moving in my life.

I decided to visit a pastor-friend who had moved from SoCal to San Francisco to pastor a church. On the return home, the Spirit spoke to me as before and stated directly, "You are going to San Francisco." Yep, you guessed it. After some time spent gathering financial support, I moved there to start an inner-city ministry. Spirit strikes again!

But before I left for San Francisco, I attended a Vineyard Christian Fellowship conference on spiritual warfare. The Spirit used this event to teach me about laying hands on people for healing, something I had never done. Totally to my surprise, Spirit orchestrated the beginning of my being healed of a terrible relationship I had with my mother (deceased), which had caused me to hold great bitterness toward her. The Spirit said, "If you are going to serve me, it's time to let those wounds heal and learn to forgive." I had never seen or experienced this kind of power before in my Christian life.

The Spirit continued to nurture my spiritual growth by leading me to a group that combined speaking in tongues together with healing. In prior years at my church in SoCal, we had never prayed for anyone's healing, let alone by speaking in tongues. Then Spirit led me to another church where I experienced Spirit in even more powerful ways (i.e., worship, prophecy, healing, tongues, discernment, intercessory prayer). The skill of learning to listen to Spirit began at that church and has never left me. The lessons I learned there were priceless and foundational.

After six years ministering in San Francisco, the Spirit called again. What?? Yes. I was traveling to support a fellow missionary who worked on ranches in Nevada. On a return trip home Spirit said, as before, "You are going to minister to ranchers." This time I knew better. I didn't quibble, disagree, or deny the call; I got ready to move. And where I landed in southeastern Oregon was totally directed by Spirit, so let me tell you that story. I think you'll see Spirit in it.

When I got the call to minister to cowboys, I thought I'd be joining my cowboy minister friends in Nevada. But I had a sense that, no, Oregon was the place. But where?

Ministry was changing for my fellow missionary cowboy friends, so they sought the direction of Spirit through a prayer team in Reno, Nevada. At the end of several hours of prayer, one of the members shared that he kept hearing the word, "Burns," but couldn't make sense of it. My cowboy friend said, "I know Burns. It's in Oregon, up Highway 395. The town isn't for me because we are committed to Nevada. But I think it's for my friend Steve."

Well, it was. Another friend of mine and I made a trip to investigate Burns as a possible launch site for my cowboy ministry. One of the first places we stopped at in Burns was a saddle shop that had an ichthus (fish) painted on the sign. When I told the proprietor why I was there, he blew me away when he said, "We've been praying for two years for a person to come and start a ministry to the ranchers and cowboys in this area." Talk about the Spirit's guidance!! And three days after moving to Burns, Oregon I started one of the first of many Bible studies in the county. The Spirit had been clearing a path for me ahead of time.

Nine years later I had a stirring (again by the Spirit) to go deeper into people's lives, to help them resolve issues that I only saw on the surface while pastoring the members of my Bible studies and two churches. And so I returned to graduate school for a Master's degree in Clinical Social Work. This led to a twenty-year practice as a mental health therapist.

My time as a therapist was not without Spirit's presence; quite the contrary. First I went on a long spiritual "journey" where, for the first time, I searched out alternative teachings and practices that I had never had the opportunity to explore before, such as meditation, Buddhism, Native American beliefs, Hinduism, Zen, Astrology, Numerology, the Tao Te Ching, and quantum physics. My fourteen-year spiritual quest was an eye-opener; many of my friends thought I had gone off the deep end and lost my faith. But I returned to a greater faith in a larger concept of God and a deeper understanding of what I've come to call the Christ-spirit, Christ-Consciousness, Christ-Light, or Christ-of-the-Universe.

This was also a time when I applied my "Spirit" experiences to my counseling, listening to Spirit for guidance regarding the healing of my patients. During part of my counseling career, I worked for about nine years with veterans deeply wounded by war. The therapeutic interventions in which I was certified were helpful, but they could not heal the spirit-soul wounds of my veteran patients. I needed a better way to work internally with my clients. This slowly led me to the study of Shamanism because Shamanism, as you will learn, is about spirit and healing. Once again, Spirit was leading, but not only for purposes of ministry; Spirit was healing me in the process.

In my study of Shamanism, I was, possibly like you, concerned that I would be asked to leave my Christian beliefs. But I discovered that wasn't the case. Shamanism is not a religion or a belief system that demands that people leave their previous beliefs and adopt different ones. I could keep Jesus right where He needed to be, as the Christ of the Universe, in the center of my life, to be worshipped as always, the One Who created all spirits in the universe, all sentient beings, with whom Shamanism was teaching me to work.

But I was curious. Though I utilized various teachings from Zen, Hinduism, the Sutras of the Buddha, and Native American perspectives, I wondered why, if the Bible was the "Word of God" as claimed, I hadn't found more content about Spirit-life and even about shamanic practices. And so I started to research the Bible, looking at it through different lenses, rather than through the lens of my rational, Western culture. Could Shamanism be found within its pages?

What I discovered is that there is a great deal in the Bible about shamanic concepts of healing, the existence and presence of helping spirits, the use of our spiritual senses and spiritual gifts, the importance of experience in understanding the Bible, remote healing, the role of vision quests, and so on. In retrospect, I was amazed at how much content the Bible offered that was not taught in churches I attended because it was considered to be too far outside what Sally and I call the orthodox "box."

As I continued my research, I began to realize that not only had I stepped out of the "box" myself, but that there were probably many Christians who were trying to do the same. In talking with other Christians, I began to see that many were looking for more power in their lives, a larger concept of Creator, or the freedom to explore what Sally and I call "universal truth" without giving up their beliefs about Jesus. I began to think that, since it takes courage to step out of the orthodox "box," if I could offer Christian people a different way to think, perhaps I might be able to help them in their personal lives as well as in their outreach of healing. Consequently, this book was developed with that goal in mind.

SALLY

My family were not churchgoers. Both parents were generous, good people, schoolteachers who were also active in the community. I was taught to abide by "the Golden Rule": Do unto others as you would have them do unto you. My family was often active in the great outdoors: camping, backpacking and gardening, which brought me joy. I learned to love and respect Earth's beauty as one of God's most refreshing and inspiring creations. Being involved in athletics taught me perseverance and focus. Being musical, I played several instruments in an orchestra and performed in both small and large choral groups. These experiences, along with school leadership roles, taught me to be comfortable addressing public audiences. International travel for pleasure and work gave me confidence in my ability to interact with people from diverse backgrounds.

My spiritual growth began when I was ten years old. Having been fascinated by a white church with a tall steeple in my small town, I told my mom I wanted to go to church there. She was surprised and asked if someone had invited me. I said, "No. I just want to go inside and see what is going on there." So, my mom would drop me off and I attended by myself for several Sundays.

It was a traditional Baptist church, so there was always an altar call at the end of services, during which the congregation sang "Just As I Am." Each week I sensed I should go forward because there was something up there I needed. One particular morning, an invisible pair of hands pulled me up by the lapels of my bright red coat and walked me down the aisle to the Pastor. He asked if I wanted Jesus in my heart and I responded "Yes!" Indeed, that is exactly what I was needing. I was baptized the following Sunday, much to the confusion of my family. God grew to become my dearest friend and I voraciously studied the Bible I was given at my baptism, digging to find direction and answers to problems and questions about my life.

While taking a short detour in my teen years, I continued my evangelical journey through adulthood and took a job at a Brethren Church I attended in Seal Beach, CA. I was pleased to utilize the knowledge and leadership skills I had acquired to teach in the classroom, in Bible studies and at various gatherings/retreats for both women and couples. On a side note, during that time I was living in a house where significant spirit activity was taking place, usually scary stuff. By necessity, I studied and sought Spirit to learn how to deal with those entities, since no one I spoke with provided a solid direction for me to take. I learned that strong spiritual boundaries ensured essential spiritual protection. To this day, I am a troubadour for helping others build these important boundaries for their safety and good health.

Years later, my involvement at church took a sharp turn after some major fallout occurred, which took place at the same time my marriage dissolved. Disappointed with so much turmoil in my life, I ended up leaving the church, but never left my love for my God.

Somewhere along the way, I became acquainted with a young woman who had grown up in a Greek Orthodox Church. Her marriage was unravelling, and she desired to re-establish her relationship with God. There was a Catholic church in my neighborhood, and although I had never attended, I felt that a church with a similar liturgy would feel more comfortable to her. So I invited her to meet up with me at a Mass.

The young woman never showed up. But as I sat through the Mass, I unexpectedly felt like I had returned home to a community where I could be spiritually nourished once again. I trained and served as a lector and was honored to bring the Eucharist/communion to the homebound. I found I loved the reverence and honor shown in the liturgy of the Mass, which was vastly different from churches I had attended in the past. While they had given me a solid Christian foundation, I felt that something was missing in a way I couldn't define. I became inspired to move outside that "box" and dive into other teachings. I began exploring other aspects of how Spirit works. I studied the lives and practices of various Catholic mystics. I joined a charismatic women's community where there was a freedom in worship I had not experienced before. As I searched for truth in areas I had previously been taught were "wrong" or "dangerous," I learned to trust my connection with God more fully, with less inhibition and judgment, knowing He would not lead me astray.

Out of the blue, I was diagnosed with a life-threatening illness. One of the wonderful ceremonies in the Catholic Church is the Sacrament of the Anointing of the Sick, and I asked to be a part of the next one offered. This ceremony cleanses and strengthens the recipient physically, mentally and spiritually to deal with their particular infirmity. As part of the ceremony, I stood at the altar and was anointed with holy oil on the top of my head, my forehead and hands in the sign of a cross. After returning to my seat, my hands began to burn where the oil had been placed and I saw green light glowing from that area. The burning was intense and went deep; it would surely leave a wound! Then, as suddenly as it began, the burning subsided and I was left wondering what had taken place.

During those years, I had changed my career focus and begun working as a Licensed Master Massage Therapist (LMT). With every client, I worked (and continue to work) with the Spirit of Wisdom, which welcomed the power to listen to the client's body to determine what is problematic. Good listening, combined with applying my intuition, resulted in alleviating pain, recognizing how physiological imbalances connect to life issues, removing and balancing blocked energies, and releasing attached entities. During some sessions, I began experiencing my hands getting very hot, so hot in fact that some clients would say, "Please remove that heating pad as it's burning me!" It was then that I realized the green mark on my hands was given to me to heal others. I had definitely found my calling to heal lives and bodies!

Throughout my twenty years of practice, I have had the honor of many profound and miraculous experiences. I continue to learn and grow as I step into opportunities to bring people into balance. One thing I've learned is that encounters with Spirit utilizing shamanic skills are always unique and tremendously effective. Shamanism is a perspective as well as a vehicle that releases us from things that bind. I have great respect for the powerful energy we have access to through Spirit, to draw people up from the depths of their suffering. It is my desire to share these insights with you so that you too can profoundly enrich the lives of those around you.

BEFORE MOVING ON, A LITTLE MORE EDUCATION ABOUT SHAMANS

We have already begun informing you about the nature of Shamanism, and now it's time to add to that picture. We want to eliminate any potential misconceptions, if any, about Shamans and Shamanism that you may have formed.

A Simple Definition of a Shaman

"Shaman (pronounced SHAH-maan) is a word from the language of the Tungus people of Siberia. A shaman is a man or woman who enters an altered state of consciousness—at will—to contact and utilize an ordinarily hidden reality in order to acquire knowledge, power, and to help other persons."[3]

There are a couple of things we learn from this definition.

First, Shamans can be either male or female; no sexism here. Second, Shamans enter an "altered state of consciousness," otherwise known as "taking a journey." A journey is much like entering a deep state of meditation. Third, the purpose of the journey is to access a "hidden reality" otherwise known to people who meditate as "the Void." And fourth, the purpose of entering the Void is to acquire knowledge and power that will enable the Shaman to help other people.

Now tell us, how strange does that sound? Be honest. The first time you ever heard the term "Shaman," you might have conjured up wild scenes of a strangely costumed indigenous man or woman, waving an exotic object, dancing half-naked around a fire all night until they collapsed in a trance. Well, maybe that happened long ago, but it is not the case for contemporary Shamans, at least none we have been around. So, what do Shamans do?

Historically, Shamans were everything to their tribes. They were the doctors because of their knowledge of plant medicine and their ability to cure various maladies, including setting broken bones. They were weather forecasters and protected their people from excessive drought or a freezing winter. Shamans told the tribe where to hunt for food, to prevent them from starving. They looked after the tribe's moral and spiritual conduct. Shamans were healers on many levels.[4]

Today's Shaman is a person driven by compassion to help his/her fellow man or woman live an abundant, healthy life in balance with others, the environment, the universe, and Creator —just like Jesus, and probably just like you. Today's Shaman, male or female, is so ordinary looking you would not be able to pick them out from a crowd!

Seven Traditional Roles of Shamans: What Shamans Do

José and Lena Stevens, noted Shamanic experts and teachers,

tell us there are seven traditional roles that Shamans have played in their communities and around the world:

- Every Shaman is trained in the ARTS. They all practice some kind of artistic, creative expression. Some of their art is used in their ceremonies. *[Jesus was a carpenter by trade. Would Jesus' healing balm of saliva and touching of lepers count as an art?]*
- Shamans are known as excellent STORYTELLERS because that's the way they imparted wisdom before books were written, conveying wisdom through their stories and myths. *[Jesus was a consummate storyteller through His parables.]*
- Shamans are HEALERS, the medicine men or women, the community's "doctors," the ones who know something about plants and cures. *[Jesus was a noted healer, one of the most powerful things He did!]*
- Every Shaman is a TEACHER. They teach because they themselves are students of life. *[Jesus was referred to as Rabbi, Teacher.]*
- Shamans are WARRIORS—less so in a fighting capacity, but more so in the sense of being fierce, courageous, and fearless to confront the grand mystery of life and the 'enemy within.' *[Remember Jesus cleansing the Temple? Certainly a "warrior" moment. And He continually resisted the establishment's Pharisee narrative by both word and action.]*
- Every Shaman is a CEREMONIALIST, that is, they create sacred space and work with groups to create whatever ceremony is needed to help the people. *[Wouldn't the Last Supper count as one of the most celebrated ceremonies ever conducted?]*
- Every Shaman is a LEADER. In ancient China, each emperor was trained as a Shaman. They have a history of being the leaders of their people."[5] *[When you think*

about it, Jesus was absolutely the quintessential shamanic leader, training His disciples who carried His teaching to the world.]

As we can see from these examples, Jesus took on every one of these shamanic roles. Even if a person does not endorse the notion that Jesus could be called an actual Shaman, His use of shamanic techniques certainly enabled Him to carry out a powerful ministry. Since Jesus is a model to us, we can learn from the shamanic tools He used and apply them in our lives and outreaches. And that's the topic to which we now turn—the shamanic practices of Jesus.

❧ 2 ❧
THE "SHAMANIC" PRACTICES
OF JESUS

Since the practice of Shamanism goes back thousands of years, is it any wonder that we find in Jesus' works a flavor of shamanic activity? It is amazing that there is such a great similarity in practices by all people who engage the spirit world and whose work derives from Spirit. Jesus was no exception. Let's take a look at some shamanic instances during Jesus' life.

JESUS' VISION QUEST: FORTY DAYS AND FORTY NIGHTS IN THE DESERT

In Mt. 4. 1-11, Jesus was led by the Spirit into the wilderness to be tempted by the devil.[1] Being led into the wilderness like Jesus is a common practice among Shamans and Medicine Men/Women. It is called a "vision quest." Multiple days are spent alone, fasting, seeking a vision and/or a spirit helper who will energize the seeker throughout their life. In Jesus' case, the "energizer" was the Holy Spirit.

People go on vision quests for a variety of reasons. Some may go to discover a power source. Others may vision quest when they need spirit-guidance, or to gain input when they sense a need to move in a new direction in life. Some use it as a time for clarification, to fine-tune their ability to hear from Spirit. Whether you call it a vision quest or a retreat, it is usually accompanied by a time of fasting that lasts a number of days. It may occur in the wilderness, on a mountaintop, or in a quiet room.

It wasn't until we began studying Shamanism in the Bible that we realized that Jesus went into the wilderness to seek a vision through an actual vision quest. Usually Life-Giver Spirit has a single theme for the person to focus on. As the hours and days progress, extraneous thoughts and concerns are stripped away by Spirit as the person concentrates more and more on the spiritual truth(s) brought to consciousness. Truth may come as an insight, a dream or vision, or an audible word. For Jesus, the deliberation was whether He would take short cuts in His ministry (offered by Satan) or follow His Father's will in its entirety, even to death.

Two of our favorite Native American medicine men (Shamans), who were both given extraordinary and powerful visions, were Plenty-Coup, chief of the Crow nation, and Black Elk, medicine man for the Oglala Lakotas. Black Elk received his vision when he was nine years old.[2] The vision is too long to present, but a short version is that Black Elk was chosen by six spiritual "grandfathers" to oversee the healing of the Lakota nation and to ensure their travel on the "red road," the path of righteousness. The vision foretold the downfall of the Lakota people, the loss of their identity, and their struggle with sickness, poverty, and death.

With the power given him by his spiritual ancestors, Black Elk was sent to heal his people and put them on the right path. He healed many people during his lifetime, was given visions that predicted the future (i.e., the coming of the hydrogen bomb years before its completion), and even had a vision of someone who strongly resembled Jesus.[3]

Plenty Coup also saw his significant vision when he was

about nine years old.[4] He dreamed that all the bison were eliminated and replaced with White men's cows. This was exceptionally disturbing not only to Plenty Coup, but to his tribal Elders, who relied on the bison for hunting, their spiritual practices and their way of life.

The Crow nation's "Wise Ones" concluded that the White men were too many to fight (contrary to other Native tribes who fought the Whites and lost). They decided to be educated by the White man and help them, as a means of insuring their tribal survival. Plenty Coup eventually became the Crow nation's chief.

Receiving visions, dreams, and instruction from Spirit are a regular part of Native American culture and spirituality. But the visitation of the Spirit to guide and powerfully change the direction of a person's life is available not just to Native American Shamans. Spirit is available to all seekers, regardless of their race or culture, who seek universal knowledge of the Spirit.

We know this to be true because in Steve's case, he traveled to the Medicine Wheel in the Bighorn Mountains in Wyoming in the summer of 2018 on a vision quest for the purpose of hearing from Spirit. Steve fasted for many days and had a powerful vision that has guided him since. He was given the energy of several powerful animals (spirit entities) to use as part of his healing mission. In his next vision quest, Steve was released by the Spirit from the attachment of a human entity which needed to move on to the Light, a very freeing experience. And in a subsequent vision quest he received very timely and powerful insights about how to navigate an important relationship.

Vision quests can be a source of very powerful experiences for those who seek the voice of the Spirit. This is what Jesus was doing in the wilderness, a very "shamanic" activity.

REMOTE HEALINGS

What is a remote healing? A remote healing is the healing of a person who is not in the healer's presence. In Mt. 8. 5-13; Lk. 7. 1-10, Jesus healed the Centurion's servant, who was not present. We typically focus on the Centurion's faith. What we don't tend to focus on is the fact that Jesus healed *remotely*, an activity that Shamans also engage in.

Think about it. Jesus was constantly surrounded by people within arm's length who were clamoring to be healed. He could have focused solely on those in need nearby. Yet on several occasions He decided to heal remotely.

Jesus not only healed remotely, He cast a demon from a girl remotely—a form of healing. A Greek woman went to Jesus and asked Him to drive a demon from her daughter. When the woman returned home, the demon had already left her daughter.[5] Again, Jesus' activity was very "shamanic" because Shamans are able to extract negative energy and entities remotely.

If you are as intrigued as we are about how remote healings occur, physics might offer us a clue. Remember Einstein's formula, $E=mc^2$? Essentially the formula means that all things in the universe are made of energy. Furthermore, quantum physicists indicate that particles may be connected even at a distance and in different locations. And they act upon one another. Based on their theories, there is strong support to believe that *everything* in the universe is energetically connected. Therefore, seeing ourselves as individual beings separate from one another is inaccurate. We, as energy-beings, are all connected (as the Buddhists and Native Americans have been telling us for centuries). Instead of viewing ourselves as separate from the person we are trying to heal remotely, we can visualize our connection to them in spirit and conduct their healing ceremony as if they were right there with us (which they are, energetically).

The point is one-ness. There is an energetic interaction that connects all of us like a giant, invisible web. What happens to you in the universe ultimately affects us all on an energy level. The thought-energy we send into the universe returns to affect not only us, but others around us as positive or negative energy. This means we can send energy to a "remote" person knowing that the other person is not "remote" at all, but connected. That person will be affected by us. "Remoteness," in that sense, is an illusion.

Let us share with you a personal example of a remote healing we were involved in. We were contacted by a local family whose nine-year-old daughter was septic and near death. She was in a coma. The girl was amazingly spiritually active at a young age and, we learned, had brought back a demonic spirit from her journeys into the Middle World (we will tell you about the Middle World later). The problem is, she had not learned how to protect herself.

We engaged in a remote healing by journeying and calling to her spirit, which was barely audible because she was so close to death. We talked to her spirit and coaxed her to fight for her own life. We could see and feel the presence of a negative spirit that had wrapped itself around her neck and was choking her. We set about remotely to remove the spirit from her and heal her body.

Several hours later we received a phone call from the girl's mother who told us her daughter had come out of her coma and was sitting up talking in bed. Once the girl had regained her health, we talked with her. We learned she had heard Sally calling to her, decided not to die, and felt the negative spirit removed from her body.

Hearing a story like that may cause some of you to be aghast that such things are possible or think that maybe we should be fearful of interacting with spirits like that. But that is exactly what Jesus did! When He gave us the right to heal at the end of Mark's gospel (Chapter 16), it included remote healing. Turns out, most of the healing we do with our clients is done remotely.

UP ON THE MOUNTAIN TO PRAY

Several times during Jesus' ministry He "went up on the mountain to pray." (Mt. 14. 23; Mk. 6. 46; Lk. 6. 12; 9. 23). It was common for Jesus to get away to pray, a very "shamanic" practice.

Steve has asked a number of pastors: "When Jesus went up the mountain to pray, what was it like for Him? What do you think He was doing up there?" Their typical answer has been: "I don't know."

Well, we don't know *exactly*. But anyone who has meditated as a common practice, or experienced shamanic journeying, had a trance/vision, or taken part in a serious spiritual retreat or ceremony where they fasted for a number of days would have a pretty good idea about what Jesus experienced on the mountain.

First, He certainly was not up on the mountain reciting prayers out of some kind of catechism. If He communed with his Father such that He said, "I and the Father are One," (John 17) then part of what Jesus experienced was what we call an "altered state of consciousness." And this altered state enabled Jesus to experience "One-ness" with the Father.

Many faith perspectives teach the difference between "ordinary time" and "non-ordinary, sacred time." Ordinary time is what we call "clock-time," time that is ruled by our physical, earthly dimensions. "Non-ordinary, sacred time" is spirit time. It is similar to that moment when we sense that time stands still, such as when we see a beautiful sunset, hold a newborn baby in our arms, feel the unconditional love of another, or come into a place where we sense sacredness.

In meditation or shamanic journeying, the spiritual part of our minds and hearts leaves the ordinary, physical world and shifts into the non-ordinary, sacred, unseen realm of the Spirit. Our spiritual senses are fully engaged, and we use our imagination to see, hear, touch, feel, smell, and sense spiritual realities. We move into different spiritual dimensions and realities. All circumstantial evidence points to the fact that Jesus was experiencing non-ordinary, sacred reality during His time on the mountain.

Think about this. When Jesus went to the mountain, He was probably exhausted. Some of His visits may have involved "resting" in the Spirit. He had to reconnect with His Father, hence the need to experience One-ness. He would have to "recharge" by reconnecting with Spirit because power was going out of/flowing from Him during His healings. And Jesus would have had to sense something about His marching orders, how to handle what was coming up in His ministry. In fact, after one visitation to the mountain He chose His twelve apostles.

Jesus was a man who was deeply, deeply, deeply connected to Spirit. He was led by the Spirit, walked in Spirit, heard from the Father in Spirit, understood in Spirit, preached and healed in Spirit, had times of rest and recuperation in Spirit, and probably had trance-like experiences in Spirit. We surmise, therefore, that some kind of altered form of consciousness was a regular part of Jesus' mountain-prayer experiences in the sacred, non-ordinary dimension that involved His contact with the Father and Spirit. The things we believe Jesus did in His time alone with Spirit are what Shamans do. They are powerful shamanic activities.

POWER OVER THE ELEMENTS

There is every reason to believe Jesus was working with "elemental spirits" when He boarded a boat and, in the middle of a storm on the Sea of Galilee, rebuked the wind and the waves, resulting in a great calm (Mt. 8. 23-26; Mk. 4. 35-41; Lk. 8. 22-25). As we observe Jesus closely, we notice that not only did He rebuke the wind and water, but He admonished the spirits as well who were churning up the wind and water. And by doing this, Jesus demonstrated His power over the spirits of the physical elements.

While Christians often use this Scripture to demonstrate

Jesus' power over His creation, we also see parallels between His actions and those of Shamans. For instance, there are many reports of Shamans working with environmental spirits in order to overcome drought, calm the wind, shift storm patterns, or redirect the flow of a river. How is this done?

Working with what we call "elemental spirits" is a shamanic activity. One of the things Shamans are noted for is talking to the spirits that inhabit the wind, rain, mountains, rivers, trees, clouds, animals, etc. Early Bible writers realized that spirits were attached to the physical elements of Earth. Later we will show you that it was the Creator who attached spirit-beings to the celestial elements of the universe (i.e., planets, stars) as well to the physical elements of the Earth.

Shamans routinely interact with the elemental spirits of the Earth, reasoning with and even instructing the spirit world. Granted, it can take a number of days for a Shaman to bring about changes to the natural elements. The Shaman must journey to inquire about the reason for the natural problem. He or she then determines from the helping spirits what solutions need to be brought to implement change. Then, while in the non-ordinary/sacred dimension, the Shaman brings into the present what they visualize as taking place in the future.

We are not suggesting that Shamans have the same power as Jesus, simply for the reason that as the incarnated presence of the Christ of the Universe, Jesus had to demonstrate unequivocal power over elemental spirits, demons, and even death (raising a number of people from the dead). Yet notwithstanding the power Jesus used as part of His mission, we believe there was a shamanic aspect to His command of the elements.

"POWER GOING OUT FROM ME"

In Lk. 8. 43-48, a woman with abnormal uterine bleeding touched the border of Jesus' garment as an act of faith, believing He would indirectly heal her. Jesus acknowledged that the woman's faith had healed her. But what we focus on here is Jesus' sense that power had gone out from Him.

We would like to view this story as a type of shamanic event. When a person is connected to Spirit through meditation, journeying, prayer, fasting, or worship, or is in touch with Spirit and operating in power, they sense the power of that connection.

Think back on the times when you attended a powerful conference or worship event, and the Spirit moved in you. Think about the last time you sensed a need to pray for someone and, when they allowed it, you began to feel your hands tingle as you placed them near the person. What about when you sensed some kind of negative energy in a person or situation and you became fortified with a sense that you needed to do something about it, to change it with the Spirit's help?

We all possess something akin to a power meter that can detect the intensity of the presence of the Spirit in our lives. When we get around people who desire healing or spiritual connection with us, we sense the urgency of their need. We feel the Holy Spirit's or our own helping spirits' power in our hands and/or bodies, or hear S/spirit[6] speak to us about what to do. We can feel power in and around us—tingling, buzzing, a deep knowing, strong premonitions, strength of character, resolve.

And it is not just Shamans. Anyone who walks in the S/spirit can tell when power is moving through them. Since learning shamanic practices and having more encounters with the Holy Spirit and our helping spirits, we have more of a tendency to operate in this capacity. We can more easily tell when "power has gone out of us" in the direction of someone's need in order to help them. It is not our power, by the way, but the S/spirit's power that we sense is going out. It has to be. None of us has power in and of ourselves. Jesus was no different. He operated by means of the Holy Spirit that flowed through Him. And again, in this sense He operated the way Shamans do.

JESUS, THE HEALER

Jesus healed for a number of reasons. Why did He heal? Because He had power; because He was fulfilling the prophecy that the Messiah would remove people's infirmities; to show His direct relationship with His Father; to release people from their infirmities caused by evil spirits and Satan; to demonstrate that He had the power to forgive sin. Jesus also healed to show the religious politicians of His day that they could not prevent Him from dispensing mercy to people with real needs when their man-made laws prohibited it on the Sabbath.[7]

The Apostle John wrote: "*God is love*, and he who abides in love abides in God, and God in him" (1 Jn. 4. 16). With a loving God and the coming of Jesus to reveal the works of the Father, is it any wonder that the most cited reason for Jesus' healing was *compassion?*[8]

While it is true that some Shamans may render their services solely for money or power, we propose that the reason most Shamans serve is out of compassion for people.

When a person commits to a daily regimen of meditation or prayer, they start to resonate with the flow of the universe, which is love. Over time, a person's spirit gets in sync with the deeper realities of life, which is the love of God. Shamans, like Jesus, commit to a lifestyle of love and compassionate acts. They resonate with the essence of the Christ-Spirit, the one we call God, or Source, or Sacred Unity. In this compassionate sense, the shamanic actions of Jesus and Shamans are the same.

JESUS, THE ULTIMATE SHAMAN

Sometimes Shamans are referred to as a "hollow bone," a conduit for the Spirit to heal. The shamanic adage is, "Get out of the way and let the helping spirits do their work."

It would be easy to link Jesus' earthly power to His divinity, but that would be a mistake. The Apostle Paul in Phil. 2. 7-8 said that Jesus temporarily set aside the "use" of His divinity in order to be fully humanized for the sake of His human mission. Rather, it seems that Jesus relied *upon the Spirit* for guidance and power.[9] The point is, if anyone was "hollow boned" it was Jesus. He "got out of the way" and let the Holy Spirit move through Him. In this way, Jesus is the Ultimate Shaman. He is the ultimate model for us.

We have provided a few examples of Jesus' shamanic actions, but we did not include all of them. There are more. Here's an idea if you are up to it. After you have read through this book, think about rereading the gospels and search out for yourself other ways that Jesus functioned shamanically. It is a great exercise.

❦ 3 ❦
TWO SOURCES OF SHAMANIC
WISDOM

THE FIRST SOURCE OF SHAMANIC WISDOM:
UNIVERSAL KNOWLEDGE GIVEN BY THE CREATOR

At this point you might be like us—the kid in the back of the class frantically waving his/her hand, trying to get the teacher's attention in order to ask THE BIG question, "Where do Shamans get their wisdom? How do they acquire it?" This is an important question, given that there are a large number of people who have an underlying suspicion that the source of Shamans' knowledge may be negative, possibly even demonic.

The good news is that the source is quite the opposite! The Book of Proverbs in the Old Testament tells us that *the one source of all true wisdom is the Lord.*

"The fear of the Lord is the beginning of knowledge..." (Prov. 1. 7). "For the Lord gives wisdom; from His mouth come knowledge and understanding" (Prov. 2. 6). See also: Prov. 8. 1-4, 15-17.[1]

The universal knowledge we talked about earlier comes from our Creator and is made available to all of humanity. This includes Shamans.

. . .

Old Testament Examples of Universal Knowledge

An example of universal knowledge being made available to Shamans is seen in the Old Testament book of Daniel (5. 11). During the reigns of Nebuchadnezzar, Belshazzar, Darius, and Cyrus, Daniel was "Chief" of the magicians, astrologers, soothsayers, and Chaldeans.[2] These "wise men" whom Daniel supervised were essentially Shamans. They sought wisdom from their earthly or celestial sources and provided it to the kings in order to help them govern their kingdoms.

Daniel was careful to point out in 2. 20-22 that God was the source of the wisdom and knowledge for these shamanic advisors. The information they received revealed "deep and sacred things" so that the advisors could have understanding and provide substantial and noteworthy offerings to the kings.

Ahhhh... Now you can breathe deeply and relax when you understand that the prime source of Shamanic wisdom comes directly from our Creator!

New Testament Examples of Universal Knowledge

The New Testament offers additional proof to show that universal knowledge was given by God to all persons, even people who did not follow Jesus. Let's start with the day of Pentecost, when the Apostle Peter quoted Joel, an Old Testament prophet, who said:

"And it shall come to pass in the last days, says God, that *I will pour out My Spirit ON ALL FLESH*; your sons and daughters shall prophesy, your young men shall see visions, your old men shall dream dreams. And on My menservants and on My maidservants I will pour out My spirit in those days; and they shall prophesy" (Acts 2. 14-18).

Part of what the Spirit does, according to Proverbs 8, is to impart wisdom to *all* who seek it. And now, Acts 2 confirms that Spirit-Wisdom is made available to *everyone* in abundance—

women and men, children, grandparents. Therefore, it is conclu-
sive that it is given to Shamans as well!

In Jesus' era, there were many examples of people who
weren't Jews or Christians who, like Shamans, were able to access
the universal knowledge given by the Spirit.

- The "many" who will come from the East and West
  (non-Jews and non-followers of Christ) and sit down
  in the kingdom of heaven with the most famous
  Jewish ancestors (Mt. 8. 11-12).
- The Centurion who exhibited uncharacteristic faith
  that exceeded the faith of the Jews during Jesus' time
  (Mt. 8. 5-13; Lk. 7. 1-10).
- The "other sheep" that Jesus spoke about. No matter
  how you interpret Jn. 10-16, even those "outside" the
  immediate fold of Jesus' followers were able to access
  universal knowledge that directed them toward God.
- Cornelius (Acts 10. 34-35). The Spirit answered his
  prayers because he represented non-
  orthodox/unchurched people who "fear (respect and
  reverence) God and whose works of righteousness
  were accepted by God."
- The Ethiopian eunuch in Acts 8. His wisdom had to
  derive from God, which allowed him to oversee the
  treasury of the queen of the Ethiopians.

All these people, like Shamans, were able to access universal
knowledge provided by the Holy Spirit, to seek wisdom from
their Creator and use their insights to benefit others.

WHAT SHAMANIC WISDOM IS USED FOR (NOT FOR THE DEMONIC)

It's not uncommon for some people who believe in Jesus to
think that Shamans are influenced by the demonic. Our teaching

above, however, counters this idea to show that Shamans tap into "Spirit" wisdom and power that is universal and given by God. They use it to serve humankind.

But let us ask you this very important question: "If Shamans' power was demonic, wouldn't they want to keep people in bondage to evil rather than to eliminate it?" This is exactly what Jesus implied when He responded to the Pharisees[3] who claimed He Himself was casting out demons by the power of Satan.

"Now when the Pharisees heard it they said, "This fellow does not cast out demons except by Beelzebub, the ruler of the demons." But Jesus knew their thoughts and said to them, "Every kingdom divided against itself is brought to desolation, and every city or house divided against itself will not stand. If Satan casts out Satan, he is divided against himself. How then will his kingdom stand?" (Mt. 12. 24-26).

Precisely our point! If Shamans respect and revere the Creator, they are not going to harm people. The wisdom Shamans receive from Spirit will be used to heal people.

And to emphasize this position, we believe that Shamans who heal are functioning in the same vein as Jesus and His followers (i.e., "the enemy of my enemy is my friend"). Remember what Jesus said in Lk. 9. 49-50:

> "Now John answered and said, 'Master, we saw someone casting out demons in Your name, and we forbade him because he does not follow with us.' But Jesus said to him, 'Do not forbid him, for he who is not against us is on our side.'"

It seems that Jesus' admonition was this: No matter what someone is doing, if it changes others for the good and accomplishes the purposes of God, do not condemn it. It appears that Jesus would approve all people who do good work. This certainly applies to Shamans.

THE SECOND SOURCE OF WISDOM GIVEN TO SHAMANS: SPIRITS BEFORE THE THRONE OF GOD, ATTACHED TO THE CREATION, WHO "HELP" SHAMANS AND US

Not only do Shamans have access to the Creator's universal knowledge given through the Spirit, they also gain knowledge and skills from another source, a very powerful source—the spirit realm.

"Helping spirits" are spirits found in the universe, and their work is to "help" humankind. They can be sensed, felt and communicated with. People often refer to them as their "Guardian Angel." It is possible for a person to have more than one helping spirit, and helping spirits do more than just "guard." Where do these spirits/helping spirits come from and are they "biblical"?

SPIRITS IN THE COUNCIL OF GOD; SPIRITS BEFORE THE THRONE OF GOD

In the Old Testament, and more specifically in the Psalms, it is taught there is a heavenly council made up of God and created, lesser "gods" (*elohim*). This assembly of holy ones surrounds the throne of God and are also called the *eliim* (heavenly beings).[4] The *elohim/eliim*[5] cannot compare with God because they are created, lesser spirit-beings. He is the Most High God.

Michael Heiser, an Ancient History and Semitic language scholar, writes the following regarding these spirit-beings: "All spiritual beings are, in biblical usage, *elohim*. All spiritual beings are members of the heavenly host, the divine council, in the sense that *they all have some role to play*. There are no spiritual beings who operate alone. They are either under God's authority or in rebellion."[6]

The number of beings in the heavenly assembly who are before the throne is incalculable, as indicated by Chapter 7 of the Old Testament book of Daniel: "...a thousand thousands, ten thousand times ten thousand..."[7] Daniel's description of the number of spirits is simply to say that it is vast.[8]

Heiser also states—and this is very important for us to understand—*"Angels are rarely named or brought to the forefront of divine activity.* Though an integral part of how Scripture shows God's will is being carried out on earth, the heavenly host's service *operates like a computer program running in the background"*[9] (italics ours).

Heiser's reasoning is this: "The emphasis of what the Bible says about the intersection of heaven and earth is, understandably, God himself."[10] So while there are exceptions—some angels are named in the Bible—the Scripture usually doesn't mention angels or their work because the emphasis is on what God is doing. But this does not mean that angels (or spirits) are not present in the biblical cosmology. They are active, but their presence is more indirectly inferred than directly stated, as we will see below.

Furthermore, Heiser indicates that the label "angel" is just a job description—a particular service rendered on God's behalf by certain members of the heavenly host. All angels, therefore, are spirit-beings. The word "angel" simply describes one of the many functions that heavenly spirit-beings perform, that of messenger. [11] And because angels (messengers) are a subset of the larger category of spirit-beings, from this point on we will no longer refer to "angels" but to the broader term of "spirits" to refer to the heavenly beings who make up the heavenly host.

WORSHIP OF THE CREATOR BY THE CREATION AND THE SPIRITS (*ELOHIM*) OF THE CREATION

We are going to explore some Bible verses regarding the Earth and the Cosmos that are very important for your understanding of what it is that Shamans access as universal knowledge. The following material is very important for you to understand and central to one of the major themes of this book. So, hang with us as we endeavor to lay out our research as simply as possible and offer you fundamentals that show how Shamanism and Christianity fit together.

Elemental Spirits of the Universe and the Earth Who Worship the Creator

Several verses in the Psalms and elsewhere reveal that elemental spirits of the Universe and Earth worship the Creator. Even animals and sea creatures venerate the Creator.

- "Oh sing to the Lord a new song! Sing to the Lord all the *earth*" (Ps. 96. 1). "Praise the Lord all you *works* of His" (Ps. 103. 22). "The *heavens* declare the glory of God, and the *firmament (sky)* shows His handiwork" (Ps. 19. 1). We ask, "Are the earth and sky capable of praising God?" Yes, says Scripture!
- Even the sun, moon, and stars praise the Lord. Ps. 148. 3-4: "Praise the Lord; praise Him *sun* and *moon*; all you *stars* of light, you *heavens* of heavens and you *waters* above the heavens (clouds)." Does the Psalmist really mean that these celestial objects can praise the Creator? Aren't they just inanimate objects? Obviously the Psalmist believes that celestial, inanimate objects can praise the Creator!
- Can we believe Isaiah when he states, "The *mountains* and the *hills* shall break forth into singing before you [the Lord], and all the *trees* of the field shall clap their hands" (Is. 55. 12)? Or, what about the Psalmist, who says: "Let the *rivers* clap their hands; let the *hills* be joyful together before the Lord" (Ps. 98. 8). It seems the creation is in a constant state of worship.
- Even *animals* voice their praise to God. "Everything that has *breath* (life), praise the Lord" (Ps. 150. 6). Rev.

5. 13 says: "And *every creature* which is in heaven and on the earth and under the earth and such as are in the sea, and all that are in them, I heard saying, 'Blessing and honor and glory and power be to Him who sits on the throne, and to the Lamb, forever and ever'" (see also Ps. 148.7).[12]

Now the question we have to answer is this: How might seemingly inanimate objects (such as the sun, moon, stars, sky, earth, mountains, hills, trees, rivers, and clouds) be able to sing the praises of God?[13] Is this just a play on words, or do Isaiah and the Psalmist really believe that these material objects and sentient creatures are capable of praising God?

Spirits Are Connected to Elements of the Earth and the Universe

In addition to the verses from Isaiah and Psalms cited above, Intertestamental/Second Temple literature such as Jubilees 2.1-2a (along with other documents not included in the Old Testament such as 1 and 3 Enoch, Tobit, Josephus, and Philo, to name a few)[14] developed a theology that connected angels [spirits] with the behavior of the skies and weather, i.e., they speak of "angels of the spirit of—fire, winds, clouds, darkness, snow, hail, frost, thunder, lightning, cold, heat, winter, springtime, harvest, and summer; and all of the spirits of His [God's] creatures which are in heaven and on earth."[15]

Michael Heiser says, "The notion that stars were animate divine beings was part of Israelite thinking. The stars had names (Ps. 147. 4), were created by God (Gen. 1. 16) and were thought to be a divine army (Judg. 5. 20; Is. 40. 25-26; Dan. 8. 10; Rev. 12. 1-9). The idea persisted well into the New Testament era."[16]

These multitudes of spirits surrounding the throne of God are in fact God's agents. They are attached to the planets, suns, moons, earth and its elements for the purpose of governing the material universe. And from what we have learned above from Isaiah, the Psalmist, and the Intertestamental/Second Temple writers, *it is these spirits attached to heavenly bodies and earthly elements who worship the Creator.*

Shamans Access the Spirits Associated with the Creation

Is this fantastic? Discovering that spirits are attached to the earth and cosmos? And if this is the first time you have been exposed to this kind of teaching, does it take your breath away? It did ours.

Of course, Shamans pick up on the presence not only of these spirits of the universe (planets and stars) but also spirits of our very own Earth—water, air, wind, fire, animals, plants, etc. Who would have thought that spirits are attached to these kinds of earthly environmental objects?

The Spirits of the Universe and Earth are Helping Spirits

Are you still with us, or have we lost you? To quickly summarize, some of the spirits who reside before the throne of God and are part of the Council of God have been attached by the Creator/Christ to cosmic and earthly elements. The role that some of these spirits are given is to help humankind, which includes Shamans and us. *That's why we call them "helping spirits."*

Noted anthropologist and founder of the Foundation for Shamanic Studies, Dr. Michael Harner, Ph.D., tells us about the relationship between Shamans and their helping spirits. He writes: "To perform his work, the Shaman depends on special, personal power, which is usually supplied by his guardian and helping spirits. Each shaman generally has at least one guardian spirit in his service, whether or not he also possesses helping spirits."[17]

Shamans use these helping spirits for wisdom, guidance, empowerment, divination, and healing. The spirits make themselves available to help Shamans and us heal ourselves, others, and our environment and to support our aspiration to rise to the highest levels of maturity.

The average Shaman, therefore, would connect with and come to rely on the help of spirits associated with their natural environment, spirits attached to elements of the universe by the Christ at creation.

It is exciting beyond belief when a person grasps the fact that spirits before the throne of God are the same ones attached to the creation and who sing the praises of their Creator. These same spirits, attached to the creation, are given the role of helping humankind and are acknowledged by Shamans as "helping spirits," who help them fulfill their shamanic functions.

We felt great joy and wonder when we made these discoveries because they gave us the theological basis to include shamanic practices within our Christian beliefs.

✲ 4 ✲
ONLY THE HOLY SPIRIT, HELPING SPIRITS, OR BOTH?

Some people may ask, "If I have the Great Spirit, why do I need helping spirits?" That is a fair question. Let's start by clarifying the word "helping." The Godhead are Supreme Beings and do not need "help." However, as Heiser says, spirits function in roles that fulfill the purposes of God, and one of God's purposes is to help human beings—ergo, they are helping spirits.[1]

A friend of ours who asked that very question works in the upper-level management of a well-known corporation, high enough to personally know the CEO. Our friend uses products created by her own corporation. We responded, "If you had a problem with a product you use that your company produces, would you call the CEO?" The answer: "No, he'd probably refer me to Customer Service." Exactly. Helping spirits are like the "customer service" division. Not only is there a division of labor in a corporation, there is a division of labor in the spirit world and in God's heavenly court. Anyone who has studied the angelic/spirit realm in the Bible knows there are echelons of spirit-being power.

As you recall from above, God oversees a heavenly court of spirit-beings. Many of you may wonder, "What does God need with a Council?" Michael Heiser replies: "The answer is just as obvious: *God doesn't NEED a council. But it's scripturally clear that He has one.*"[2]

In a way, one might say that God is like a CEO, overseeing a large organization of spirits, who have different functions. Some of the spirits have been given to us to help us in our healing work. Thus, we call them "helping spirits."

We also can call the CEO's Vice President, Jesus (so to speak), or Chief Energy Officer (the Holy Spirit, so to speak). But the "corporation" has other departments, personnel (spirits), and tools which the CEO has put in place in order to help us get our job done.

Here's our logic: if God does not need the "help" of spirits but uses them, and if Jesus does not need the "help" of His Body (the Church) but uses us as His arms and legs, is it safe to believe the Holy Spirit also uses spirits while not "needing" them? Yes.

While admittedly the Scripture does not directly indicate that there is a division of labor, we believe it is safe and rational to believe that such is the case. Furthermore, we believe the work of helping spirits is under the authority and direction of the Godhead, especially by the Holy Spirit.

There is nothing to keep us from calling on the Spirit. But, if there is a division of labor, why not also draw on the help of spirits who are available if they are loyal to God and part of the overall operation of the Holy Spirit? Why not use as many resources as possible? It's been our experience that helping spirits make themselves available to help us, which helps them fulfill their purpose.

But let's be clear about this. Just because we access helping spirits does not mean we worship them. That would be idol worship, and worship is reserved only for those deserving of worship: Creator, Christ-Spirit, and Lifegiver (Holy) Spirit.

SPIRITS "OF GOD" WHO ARE AVAILABLE TO HELP US

The issue, therefore, is not whether helping spirits exist; they do. The issue is whether spirits submit to Creator's authority and purposes to serve us. That is precisely why the Apostle John made such a specific statement regarding spirits: "Dear friends, do not believe every spirit, but "test the spirits" to see whether they are *of God*" [. . . or not—our insertion] (1 Jn. 4. 1).

The Apostle's statement makes it clear that while there are spirits who are *"not of God,"* there are spirits who are "of God," and not in rebellion. These are the spirits whom Shamans access and who are available to assist us as well if we ask.

OUR POSITIVE EXPERIENCE WITH HELPING SPIRITS

The helping spirits we participate with are powerful and too useful to ignore. We have many stories of how our helping spirits provided us with information which was used to help or heal our clients. Here are two quick stories that illustrate how our helping spirits connected us energetically with the needs of our clients.

JOHN

John called to ask for help. For an unknown reason, he had developed a deep muscular infection in his right thigh. Treatment required not only the use of powerful antibiotics, but the removal of a significant portion of John's thigh muscles in order to eliminate the infection. But even more problematically, John's doctor's grave concern was that the remaining infection could travel up his leg and infect his hip implant. The result would be catastrophic, requiring surgeons to remove John's hip replacement, immobilizing him with no hip joint until the infection could be eliminated. Can you imagine having no hip joint in one of your legs?

We worked on John remotely. We called on our helping spirits who showed us how to extract the infection energetically and put a protective barrier around John's hip. The good news is that the barrier worked, the antibiotics did their job, and John was able to walk again.

A reader might respond, "Well, it was really the antibiotics that got him better, not the Shaman mumbo-jumbo." But working with helping spirits is always a surprise and they have a way of confirming to us that our energetic work is effective. The rest of the story goes like this.

While we were engaged in our remote healing ceremony, Sally had a vision of an eagle in her mind's-eye, flying over a river which moved through a canyon filled with dense trees on the sides. The vision came out of nowhere and was a total surprise. When Sally shared her vision with John later on, he told her that while he was in Vietnam (two tours), during times of anxiety he would call on the eagle to protect him.

By the way, John is part Cheyenne Indian. The eagle is one of the most sacred and powerful symbols and allies of his tribe. John told Sally he'd never shared his practice of calling on the eagle with anyone. And it was a surprising confirmation of our work with him. Amazing synchronicities!

JAY

Jay was led to contact us about a negative spirit that inhabited a home on his family's property. The entity caused a darkness to fill part of the house. The entity negatively influenced family members to yield their lives to substance use and anxiety. A foul odor emanated from the area inhabited by the spirit. No amount of cleaning would remove the stench. Even the family dogs steered clear of that specific area in the house.

When we journeyed, Sally saw blood. Steve sensed a murder had been committed many years previously, possibly before the house had been built.

With subsequent journeys, Steve came to sense that the land had to be cleansed by the tribal entities that had inhabited the land when the murder was committed. Steve's helping spirits arranged for the spirits of the Abenaki tribe to do a cleansing ceremony. With their amazingly colorful regalia, which Steve observed in his mind's-eye during a journey, the Abenaki engaged in a sacred ceremony and removed the power and negative effect of the shed blood. The cleansing enabled us to work with the negative entity and move it on in its spiritual trajectory. With the spirit gone, the odor vanished and the house took on a fresher, cleaner sense.

As with the story of John above, synchronicities occurred that confirmed the healing had been completed. When Steve and Sally visited Jay's home in person, they sensed that the home was clear. But additionally and in her mind's-eye, Sally saw a woman standing near where the negative entity had been located. The woman was beautifully dressed, exuded contentment, and was happy that all the guests were enjoying the gathering at the house—definitely a sign that all was made well.

Our conclusion, both biblically and from experience, is that healing spirits are positive entities, available to help and guide. The healings that arise from the powerful assistance of these spirits is phenomenal. We and our clients have benefitted tremendously from our interaction with these wonderful helpers.

The helping spirits we access fill a multitude of roles. They:

- Protect us from negative entities.
- Show us when and how to deal with a malevolent spirit.

- Help us banish (exorcise) a malevolent spirit from a person.
- Reveal the source of a person's illness.
- Indicate the way we should proceed with a person's healing, which might be physical, psychological, emotional, or spiritual.
- Move through us to accomplish a healing.
- Give us words/information about a person or their problem we would not have known otherwise.
- Help us navigate the spirit world.
- Teach us in simple and direct ways about the spirit world.
- Affirm that Jesus is Lord.

WHY ARE HELPING SPIRITS NOT MENTIONED MORE IN THE NEW TESTAMENT?

Before closing this chapter, we need to ask: Why is there not more mention of spirits in the New Testament when they are mentioned in the Old Testament/Intertestamental literature? Most New Testament references to "spirit" are negative and refer to deceiving spirits, lying spirits, and demons.

Michael Heiser says that by the time the New Testament was written, the focus had shifted to Christ, who came to defeat the powers of darkness (Heb. 2. 14-15).[3] Because good spirits were already acknowledged as active and working, there was no need to further develop a theology of angels or spirits in the New Testament; it was already established. So there was no need to mention "spirits" unless they were attached to Satan as "deceiving spirits" or demons, whom Jesus came to defeat. Nevertheless, helping spirits were still working in the background of the New Testament times and they are still working today to help Shamans and us in our healing practices.

🝊 5 🝊
THE WORLD AS SHAMANS AND CHRISTIANS SEE IT. WHO IS RIGHT?

Have you ever noticed how people confuse themselves? For some reason, we humans tend to prefer an "either-or" outlook to a "both-and." We prefer to select only one option from several instead of seeing the possibility that several options could be "true" at the same time. Perhaps if we see things as black and white, life is easier to understand.

We potentially find ourselves in this kind of situation, thinking we must "choose" between the validity of Shamanistic or Christian worldviews. But we have to ask, "Why must Shamanism and Christianity be competitive with each other when it is not the objective of Shamanism to "win" or to be viewed as superior?" In fact, Shamanism can function right alongside a Christian viewpoint and assist as a wonderful aid.

THE THREE WORLDS OF SHAMANISM

You see a cowboy and you assume he/she knows something about horses or cows. You see a nurse and you think that he/she must have some kind of medical training. You see a Shaman and . . . ??? You are not sure how to think about them. So let's take this time to get an even deeper look at Shamans, their history and worldview.

Shamans, for us, are the original practitioners who live in indigenous cultures. Shamans, whether men or women, are mentored in their own rural cultures in areas such as in Ecuador, Peru, the Amazon, or even in a Native American tribe. They are the real McCoys![1]

When you visualize the areas in which most Shamans live, you can understand how their rural setting influences the way they view reality. In their belief system, the world is divided into three parts, a Lower, a Middle, and an Upper World. This worldview is remarkably consistent among Shamans the world over.

The Lower World

We sometimes describe the "world down there" as a negative place (i.e., hell). However, for a Shaman, the Lower World is a beautiful world filled with animals, plants, trees, insects, rocks, etc. It is the physical world, the physical environment; it is nature. If you were to magically extract all humans from the planet, what would be left is the Lower World, which extends down into the depths of the Earth.

What is important to understand about Shamans is that they consider spirits to be connected to and within everything. This makes sense, because everything in creation was birthed by the Creator-Spirit. Therefore, elements in the earth and the universe had spirits attached to them by the Creator, or the Creator filled all living things in the Lower World, right down to the tiniest organisms, with its essence or spirit. Shamans, therefore, access the many spirits that are part of the environment where they live. To them, the "Lower World" is brimming with spirit in everything they see, hear, taste, and touch.

Because Shamans connect with the spirit-energy—the same energy the Chinese refer to as chi—found in their environment, they sense it, talk to it, gather it, and use it to give them wisdom and power for things such as healing. Part of the energy used for healing can come from the Lower World.

A very common form of Lower World energy that Shamans use comes from animals. Certain animal energies present themselves differently to each Shaman. These are referred to as "Power Animals" or the Shaman's "totem." Shamans do not access the spirit of an actual animal per se, they draw on the energetic qualities of the species (such as its speed, tenacity, sight, intelligence) in the form of its spirit. Many helping spirits offer their characteristics to Shamans and us as represented by an animal.

In our workshops we teach our participants how to identify at least one power animal who becomes available to them for protection and assistance.

Sometimes Shamans journey to the spirit realm of the Lower World to perform various functions. They do this by traveling into what might be interpreted as a virtual Earth. It is there they can derive wisdom from the Earth ("Mother Earth"). We will explore this further in Part Two.

The Middle World

Shamans view the Middle World as consisting of both humans and human-spirits. Shamans journey into the spirit realm of the Middle World to carry out a variety of transactions for humans. Part of the ethics that govern Shamans, or shamanic practitioners, is not to interact with a human's spirit without first obtaining that person's permission.

One aspect of interacting with Middle World spirits pertains to dealing with the spirits of persons who have passed on. It is a common belief that a human spirit, upon leaving their body at death, immediately moves toward the light and life of the Upper World. Christians cite Heb. 9. 27 as an example of this: "It is appointed for man to die and then the judgment." Experience, however, has proven to us that it may take a little longer for a human spirit to find its way to a "judgment" (or what we now know from near-death experiences [NDEs] as a life review). In other words, there are instances in which it may take a little longer for a person's soul/spirit to transition to the Upper World than we assume.

For instance, some spirits get "stuck" in the Middle World for various reasons. It is not uncommon for the spirits of people who have been involved in an accident, where death was immediate, to be suspended in a state of shock. "What just happened to me?" they wonder. "Where am I?" Because certainly their perception and senses have radically changed in a matter of seconds. Their spirit is outside their body and they may experience a sense of being lost, frustrated, or even angry. Their spirit lingers in a state of confusion or ambivalence. These spirits may attach to the geographical area where they exited their physical body, such as at an accident site.

For some people who have passed, their spirits are just not ready to move on to the afterlife of the Upper World. They may strongly believe they need to stay around to fulfill an important task, or are obliged to watch over someone they believe is dependent on them. Perhaps they may be frightened of the afterlife, which is often common considering the stigma our culture places on death and the dying process. Sometimes, for the purpose of self-comfort, a spirit will seek out and attach themselves to a relative with whom they have shared a positive relationship. The relative is not "possessed" but may occasionally feel the presence or energy of something close by that feels odd. Without knowing it, the relative may have inherited an attaching spirit of a deceased family member or friend (not to freak anyone out, but this does occur).

In all of these cases, when a spirit gets stuck in the Middle World and cannot move on to the Upper World, a Shaman can help by performing a role called a "psychopomp." The word "psychopomp" literally means "guide of the soul." The Shaman, with the spirit's permission, aids in ushering the spirit to the Upper World.

Psychopomp work is absolutely fascinating and somewhat unbelievable to anyone who has never heard of it before. And before we were exposed to Shamanism, we also would have found the concept to be incredulous. But . . . we have performed some psychopomp work and find it to be a most amazing process. Take our word for it!

The Upper World

So again, think of an indigenous male or female Shaman. Imagine them coming out of their rustic habitation and looking up into the sky. Where else, they might think, would a human spirit or soul go into the afterlife but UP, UP, UP?

For a Shaman, the Upper World is the place where the spirits of humans go when they pass and move toward the famous "Light" we hear about from NDEs. It is the place where their ancestors are. It is also where the Creator dwells, if they consider the Creator to be a Spirit separate from the Creation itself. And where the Creator dwells, so also do many of the helping spirits, especially those associated with celestial objects. The Upper World is the place to go to receive wisdom from ancestors, helping spirits, spirits of the cosmos, and the Creator.

There is a vague reference to "ancestral" spirits in Heb. 12. 1: "Therefore, we also, since we are surrounded by so great a cloud of witnesses . . ." Some people would place Catholic saints, often sought for their intercessory help, in this category. Great figures of history are to be found in the Upper World such as Mary, the Mother of Jesus; Buddha, Moses, Mary Magdalene, etc. Angels are also associated with the Upper World.

Shamanic Functions in the Three Worlds

Achieving the shamanic state of altered consciousness

enables Shamans to journey to these three worlds (Lower, Middle, and Upper). Shamans draw power from elements of the Earth, nature, and the universe. They also listen to, interact with, and draw power from the spirits of the Lower and Upper worlds in order to perform their various functions. These functions may include: helping disembodied, Middle World spirits cross to the Lower or Upper Worlds (psychopomp); extraction of non-sentient, negative energy; de-possession of sentient Middle World spirits; power soul retrieval; divination; power restoration; and connecting people to their helping spirit(s)/power entity(ies). We will define each of these in Part Two, Chapter Twelve: Advanced Shamanic Practices.

THE WORLD OF THE BIBLE—JESUS, HIS MISSION, AND HIS CHURCH

While the world of the Bible could not be more different from a Shaman's world of Lower and Middle World spirits, the people of Jesus' era did conceive of a cosmology that strongly resembled the cosmology of shamanic, indigenous peoples. The Hebrew concepts of an Underworld, the Earth, and the Heavens line up in roughly the same manner. The similarity of "worlds" probably occurred because the people of Jesus' time were indigenous, rural people as well.

The cosmology differs between Shamans and Jesus in that Jesus seemed to deal only with demonic spirits, not Middle World spirits (unless demons can be considered Middle World spirits). Shamans, on the other hand, deal only with Middle World spirits and not demons (as we were informed by some of our shamanic mentors).

Jesus' need to cast out demons was central to His mission. Let's examine why. According to Christian theology, there has been a cosmic battle taking place in the heavenly realms since the universe began. It is a battle between good and evil, between God and some of the spirits He created. These are overarching themes that run in the background of the Bible but inform the purpose for which the Bible was written.

We have mentioned the existence of a council of heavenly beings under the leadership and authority of the Creator. Strange as it may seem, some of these beings are hostile to the purposes of God.

One additional and important piece of information is that God put some of these "council" entities/spirits/angelic beings (defined by the Apostle Paul in Eph. 6. 12 and Col. 1. 16; 2. 15) in charge of the spiritual governance of the Earth's nations (Dt. 32. 8). They are known in the Bible as Principalities, Powers, World Rulers, Spiritual Forces, Thrones, Dominions, Names, and Strongholds. Many, however, rule for the sake of their own power, against the will of God, and even conspire with Satan. (The endnote is extensive and worth reading with regard to this topic. [2])

The picture of reality, according to the Bible, is that the battle being fought in the heavens was brought to Earth with the creation of humankind. In fact, the battle is being fought over who has control of humankind. The Bible teaches that Jesus and His Church are central figures in this struggle. The Apostle Paul depicts this drama for Jesus' Church in Ephes. 6. 10-13.

According to these verses, one of the sources of evil coming against Jesus and His Church was (and still is) the rulers of the darkness of this age, one of whom is Satan and his demonic forces of darkness. This is the reason that Jesus, in His ministry, cast out a great number of demons.[3] Jesus had to clearly demonstrate His authority as the Son of God over the powers of darkness, and to free people from bondage. Jesus also showed by His death and resurrection that the end was starting for Satan and his dominions.

SO, MIDDLE WORLD SPIRITS AND DEMONS: WHICH WORLDVIEW IS RIGHT?

While the Bible does not refer to Middle World disembodied spirits, speaking only of evil unclean spirits, it doesn't mean that Middle World spirits do not exist. Many people might think this has to be an "either-or" situation, but in actuality both are right at the same time. And just because some Shamans may not believe that demons exist does not mean they don't.

The takeaway is this. If Christians acquired shamanic tools, they could help people by extracting/de-possessing them of unwanted, negative energies and Middle World spirits. And because Jesus gave His followers His authority and power over demons as a continuation of His ministry (Lk. 10. 19), the same Christian could be effective in freeing people from demonic bondage as well. We need the Christian church and shamanic tools to heal and empower people using both processes. These tools would make a Christian very powerful in dealing with the spirit realm and helping humankind.

So who is "right"? Both. And wonderfully so.

Sally and Steve's experience

We have dealt with both demonic spirits and Middle World human-spirits who had not crossed over. A demonic spirit had put melanoma cancer on the wife of a friend. When we remotely de-possessed her, the spirit threatened us, separately, telling us that it would harm not only us but our families. The threats did not work because we moved the dark spirit on to another dimension where it could no longer hurt anyone.

We helped the Middle World human spirits attached to two of our friends pass on to the Upper World. One of the spirits was reluctant to go but eventually took the opportunity to pass over. The other spirit was old and tired and went easily into the Upper World.

This is a case where our experience with the Bible and Shamanism overlap. We don't deny the reality of darkness which the Bible presents any more than we deny the experience we have of dealing with Middle World spirits. Both experiences are very real and very true. We are glad we have both sets of "tools" to use.

THE AUTHORITY OF CHRIST GIVEN TO US

There is no doubt that dealing with the demonic is not pleasant. But the instances when we encounter them are extremely infrequent. Still, if you were in a situation where this might occur, it is good to know not only the technique for handling a dark spirit but also your authority in dealing with such an entity. We want to address this before moving on to the next chapter.

Let's start by saying that while we use shamanic skills and helping spirits as part of our service of healing, we do not put Christ-Jesus on a par with the helping spirits or any spirit in the spirit realm whom we call on to assist us.

THE CHRIST-SPIRIT INCARNATED IN JESUS

Regarding the Christ-Spirit, whom we refer to as the Christ-of-the-Universe, Christ-Spirit or Christ-Light, the Apostle Paul stated in Col. 1. 16-17:

"For by Him all things were created that are in heaven and that are on earth, visible or invisible, whether thrones or dominions or principalities or powers. All things were created through Him and for Him. And He is before all things, and in Him all things consist."

Jn. 1. 1-5 and Phil. 2. 5-7 make it quite clear that the Christ of the Universe, who created all things, incarnated in the man Jesus.

Furthermore, the Apostle Paul said of Jesus, that because He died on the cross:

"Therefore God also has highly exalted Him and has given

Him *the name which is above every name,* that at the name of Jesus every knee should bow, of those in heaven and of those on earth, and of those under the earth, and that every tongue should confess that Jesus Christ is Lord, to the glory of God the Father."

The previous verses indicate our belief that Christ-Jesus is above all spirits in the spirit-hierarchy/chain of command in the heavenly and earthly realms: cherubim, seraphim, *elohim* in the Council of God, angels, archangels, helping spirits, principalities, powers, dominions, demons, etc. All spirits must submit to Him. His name is above every name.

We believe this reality is very important when working in the spirit realm. If a Christian who practices Shamanism does not know in whose power and authority they are working, then it becomes a game of "my helping spirit is bigger than yours," which is bound to fail, with possibly serious consequences.

For example, there are spirits out there who are higher up the spirit-hierarchical chain and more powerful than some of our helping spirits. They may choose not to submit to the authority of our helping spirits. But if in our Christian belief we know in Whom we put our faith and in Whose power we work, then we have God's authority to state directly to any spirit that we come in the authority and power of Christ-Jesus and command them to leave.

There is also a caveat for anyone who might speak the name of Jesus to a demon for purposes of de-possession without having a true belief in Jesus. The seven sons of Sceva were a perfect example of this (Acts 19. 11-16). They attempted to exorcise an evil spirit by using "Jesus" in name only. The man in whom the evil spirit dwelt leaped on them, overpowered them, and beat them. Not a good outcome.

After His resurrection Jesus stated about Himself in Mt. 28. 18: "All authority and power has been given to Me in heaven and on earth," and He has given His authority and power to us. We can rest assured that as followers of Christ all spirits must submit to our intention and the intention of the helping spirits with whom we are working. When our intentions are in line with the purposes of Christ, especially when we are dealing with a demonic element, we know that we stand as agents of the exalted Christ-Jesus, who is above every name and power.

6

FROM THE BIBLICAL MAP TO
THE SPIRITUAL TERRAIN AND
BEYOND

L et's take a moment and recap. What we have discovered so far paints a very positive picture of Shamans and what they do.

- They connect with the Proverbs' Spirit that is available to all humankind. The same natural laws that science studies are the same natural laws which give rise to shamanic spiritual practices—general spirit-laws of the universe created by God.
- Shamans cross into the unseen, non-ordinary, sacred realm to access helping spirits found in creation who want to benefit humankind and guide the Shamans to bring healing.
- Shamans use their spiritual perception, insight/intuition, and practices to heal and benefit humankind.

Would you have come to those conclusions on your own? Maybe, or maybe not. After all, Shamans do not have the best of reputations among Christians. Much of this is due to Old Testament passages in Leviticus, Deuteronomy, and Numbers, which we will address in the next chapter. But for now, we want to go in a slightly different direction that has to do with the way people use or don't use experience to help them interpret the Bible.

People in the Christian faith get a little nervous when the conversation turns to using experience to deepen their understanding of the Bible. After all, they would respond, the commands of the Bible are quite clear and do not require the help of experience to interpret them.

But we are talking about more than following Scriptural commands. What we are addressing here is using our Bible knowledge, coupled with our spiritual experiences, in order to expand our understanding of and interaction with spiritual realities. In other words, a person can cite chapter and verse, but that does not necessarily mean the person has experienced the deeper spiritual realities to which the Bible is pointing. Our belief is that the Bible is directing us to a deeper, spirit-"experience" rather than just a black-and-white, rational, intellectual knowledge of Scripture.

We'll use an analogy to make our point. If you were on a hike and using a map to guide you to a destination, you could spend all your time memorizing the features of the map. But that would not be enough to get you to your goal. At some point, you would have to put the map down and start looking at and interacting with the actual, physical terrain. The map is no substitute for actual feet on the ground.

This holds true for our spiritual life. Scriptures (the map) show that spirits exist and can be of help to us. But it is not enough to know this intellectually. Ultimately, we need to experience them by putting our "Bible-map" down and walking the path with them. When we do this, our spirit-experience reciprocates to expand our biblical knowledge and broaden our understanding of the biblical contexts.

Sally and Steve's Experience

To determine whether helping spirits exist and are "helpful," we researched Scripture to verify that spirits are real and are "of God" (available to help us). Then, we used shamanic techniques to journey extensively in order to encounter these spirits. In the process, not only did we confirm the presence of spirits and the spirit realm but we learned that our "helping" spirits do a number of beneficial things for us. They empower, protect, offer guidance and wisdom, heal, and give us claircognizance (the ability to acquire psychic knowledge without knowing how or why you know it) and clairvoyance (to perceive things or events in the future), to name a few.

We have to admit, experiencing the spirit realm has not always been easy. It has taken a lot of practice. And moving into that realm has been something akin to swimming upstream when we talk to our friends about our studies and experiences. Swimming upstream has been necessary for two reasons. First, our Western, rational culture prefers us to focus our senses solely on the physical, material world. And second, there are many churches that do not validate experiences of the spirit realm for a variety of reasons. The result is that many people are left trapped in their physical dimension (the "map" of the Bible) whereas the Bible repeatedly points to an experience in the S/spirit dimension as a way of life (the "terrain"). Jesus said: "God is Spirit, and those who worship Him must worship in spirit and in truth," (Jn. 4. 24).

TURNING ON OUR SPIRITUAL SENSES

In the following passages, it is clear that Jesus expected His followers to go beyond their physical senses and use their spiritual senses to perceive the spiritual realities happening around them, to use their "eyes to see and ears to hear." Jesus wasn't talking about peoples' physical eyes and ears. He grew upset with them when they didn't make the effort. For instance, Jesus had to ask His disciples in Mk. 4. 13, "Do you not "see-to-perceive" (*oida/eido*) the meaning of this parable? (If not), how then will you come to understand all the (other) parables?"

In Mk. 7. 17-18, Jesus had to explain to His disciples the meaning of being defiled from the inside out. He asked them, "Are you thus without understanding also?" Another way of translating "without understanding" is "foolish" or "stupid." Jesus could have been asking His disciples, "Are you that out of it that you can't figure out my teaching? Think about it!"

In Mk. 8. 17-21, the disciples confused Jesus' reference of the leaven (teaching) of the Pharisees with failure to bring bread on a trip. He asked them, "Do you not yet perceive and understand (put two and two together)?" And Jesus added, "Is your heart still *hardened?*" The Greek word for "hardened" is *poróo*: covered with a thick skin, calloused; to make the heart dull; to lack understanding. Hardened since when? Since Mk. 6. 52, because the disciples hadn't figured out that bread was not the issue; Jesus could multiply it on demand. Then Jesus asked, "Having eyes, do you not see?" (*blepo*— see spiritually). "Having ears, do you not hear?"— hearing with understanding. "How is it you do not understand"?

The disciples could not grasp the fact that Jesus and His ministry were as much *spiritual* as *physical*. They kept trying to reason things in the physical when He was trying to take them beyond to perceive the spiritual realities at work in His person and work. Or to use our earlier analogy, Jesus' disciples kept looking at their map. But Jesus was trying to take the map out of their hands for a bit and get them to "look up" and experience the spiritual realities happening around them. Their "spiritual" experiences were supposed to inform their thinking and their interpretation of what they were experiencing physically.

LOOKING DEEPER

One of our favorite stories in the Bible is found in 2 Kgs. 6. 15-17. The servant of the prophet Elisha saw that the Syrian army had completely surrounded their city with horses and chariots. Death was imminent! He only saw the physical world and used his physical senses to interpret reality. And appropriately, the servant became deathly afraid.

Elisha, on the other hand, used his spiritual senses to perceive a whole different reality. Elisha prayed to the Lord to open the eyes of the servant, who, when he looked again with his spiritual eyes open, was able to see that "the mountain was full of horses and chariots of fire (angels/spirit-beings) all around Elisha." Wow! What a sight! Elisha and his servant were totally protected by the spirits that surrounded them.

These verses are a challenge to us all. The question becomes, "What reality do we wish to see?" "What kind of reality do we want to experience?" Do we want to see only the physical chariots and horses, or the horses and chariots of fire (spirits) in the spirit realm? That's the decision we all have to make.

Let us ask you a question: Are you not "seeing or hearing" because you haven't turned on your spiritual senses? Are you like the servant of Elisha? Are you afraid to step out of the box that limits your spiritual understanding and experience because you cling to the "map" of the Bible and haven't moved beyond chapter and verse to the spirit-experiences to which it points? Or perhaps you "see and hear" but want to know more.

EXPERIENCE BRINGS UNDERSTANDING, UNDERSTANDING COMES FROM THE HEART

In Mt. 13. 15, Jesus stated we "understand" with our hearts. Shamans teach in the same manner. They say that our minds lead us into illusion, to be confused by the physical world instead of seeing true truth in the Spirit and with our hearts.

José Luis Stevens, world-renowned writer, shamanic teacher and practitioner writes,

"The false personality is a pretend consciousness that relies on the perception of separation in order to maintain its storyline. It lives off the vitality of Spirit by distorting its message and diverting it to its own aims and goals."

"The favorite activity of the false personality is distraction. The favorite tool of the false personality for creating distraction is *thought*: endless thoughts explaining, comparing, judging, processing, analyzing, figuring, considering, denying, agreeing, arguing, blaming, identifying, and on and on. Humans have elevated thought to the golden throne and proclaimed it king. Yet thought can be a huge troublemaker when it is separated from its source, the higher mind that resides in the heart."[1]

We find our way back to our "heart" when we use the Bible (our thought-map) as a jumping-off point into the experiential world of Spirit and trust that the Spirit will guide us into all truth (Jn. 16. 13). We must agree to do this with our hearts, otherwise we will never "see, or hear, or understand." Once we understand our spiritual experiences with our hearts, we use those experiences to help us interpret our beliefs and holy books in a broader sense and find their deeper spiritual meaning.

Do you remember when you first read or heard about Jesus multiplying bread and fish to feed 5,000 people? Maybe you saw yourself multiplying the bread at the second feeding of the 4,000, when Jesus said to His disciples, "You feed them." You saw yourself stepping forward in faith and saying, "Yes Lord, I will." That is what we are talking about here, us becoming S/spirit doers as we jump off the pages of our sacred books, our doctrines, or our catechisms, into direct spirit-experiences because our spiritual senses are turned on! You get it! You want to be right there with Jesus, helping Him do His miracles. And so do we. Let's continue on.

7

DIVINATION FOR THE SAKE
OF HEALING

A belief (false) prevails in some conservative circles that Shamanism must be bad because it practices divination and acts as a medium to spirits. This is understandable to those who are familiar with the following verses in the Old Testament:

- Lev. 19: 26, 31: "You shall not eat anything with the blood, nor shall you practice divination or soothsaying!" (v. 26); "Give no regard to mediums and familiar spirits; do not seek after them to be defiled by them" (v. 31).
- Lev. 20: 6: "And the person who turns to mediums and familiar spirits, to prostitute himself with them, I will set my face against that person and cut him off from his people."
- Lev. 20. 27: "A man or a woman who is a medium, or who has familiar spirits, shall surely be put to death; they shall stone them with stones. Their blood shall be upon them."
- Dt. 18: 9-14: "When you come into the land which the Lord your God is giving you, you shall not learn to

follow the abominations of those nations. There shall not be found among you anyone who makes his son or his daughter pass through the fire, or one who practices witchcraft, or a soothsayer, or one who interprets omens, or a sorcerer, or one who conjures spells, or a medium, or a spiritist, or one who calls up the dead."

A surface reading of these verses might give anyone a strong negative reaction to Shamanism. But let's take a deeper look to see what was taking place when these verses were written and whether they apply to modern-day Shamanism.

In the books of Exodus, Deuteronomy, Leviticus, and Joshua, God (Yahweh) took a rag-tag group of people (the twelve tribes) who had lived in Egypt for 430 years and attempted to shape them into a nation that looked only to Him for leadership as their One true God.

The Israelites' rejection of idols ("strange gods") did not happen overnight!! Within a short period after embarking on the Exodus and with Moses up on Mt. Sinai receiving the ten commandments, the Israelites became fearful and quickly returned to their idols (Ex. 32). Later, even after wandering in the desert for 40 years under the Lord's protection and provision, Joshua had to exhort the Hebrews to put away their foreign gods as they were about to enter the Holy Land (Jos. 24. 23).

God's plan was that His people, the nation of Israel, would be "holy, set apart to Me." Since God would appoint His prophets to speak His words to the people (Dt. 18. 18), there would be no need for the services of the mediums, soothsayers, magicians, necromancers, spiritists, etc. that were operating in that day. Rather, God would make His will known directly to His people through His spokespersons, the prophets, who "divined" the "secret counsel" of God through God's Spirit (Neh. 9. 30; Zech. 7. 12; Amos 3. 7).

The reality was that God's prophets, as His mediums and

diviners, operated in a manner similar to the non-Israelite soothsayers, magicians, necromancers, and spiritists. It's just that they
were the "authorized" version, "*God's*" seers and messengers,
"divining" both the future punishment that awaited Israel if they
failed to do what they were told, as well as the blessings they
would receive if they complied.

There's a deeper reason, however, why God would not allow
His people to use the services of the local mediums, soothsayers,
diviners, necromancers, spiritists, etc. in those days (Dt. 12. 30).

THE MEDIUMS AND SEERS OF THE
CANAANITES/AMORITES WERE CORRUPTED BY
DARK FORCES

In the internet article, *The Abominations of the Canaanites*, Pastor
David Padfield sets forth a comprehensive list of the "abomina-
tions" which the Canaanites/Amorites committed and which the
Lord abhorred.[1]

Padfield says the Canaanite deities had no moral values other
than promoting material prosperity, physical satisfaction, and
human pleasure. Therefore, in a sense, anything was a "go" even
if it involved burning children for worship, examining animal
entrails, consulting the dead, using magic to alter the course of
events, male/female prostitution, sorcery, bestiality, murder,
promiscuity, or divination as fortune-telling.

It is easy to conclude from what Padfield tells us that the
Principalities and Powers, put in place by God to govern the
Canaanite nation for good (Dt. 32. 8), were evil spirit-beings.
They used their positions of authority and power to morally
corrupt the people and draw the people's allegiance to themselves. The "spirits" that were accessed through divination (fortune-telling), magic, sorcery, and necromancy were spirits of
darkness, doing the bidding of the rulers of darkness, the spiritual overseers of Canaan.

It is a fact that Shamans, indeed, engage in divination and

transact with helping spirits. So should we automatically conclude that anyone who engages in divination is on the path to destruction? That conclusion would be wrong. Fortune-telling is only one aspect of divination. Divination also can involve "future-telling or foretelling," which is different. Future-telling or foretelling is also known as prophecy or prophesying.[2]

JESUS' "DIVINATION"

There are many occurrences of acceptable "divination" (future-telling, prophecy) demonstrated in the Bible. Divination as future-telling or foretelling was one of the prophetic functions. As the ultimate prophet, Jesus spoke prophetically and foretold: His death, the destruction of the temple and Jerusalem, the end times, Peter's denial, Peter's death, the upcoming persecution of His disciples, and Judas' betrayal.[3]

OLD AND NEW TESTAMENT PROPHETS' "DIVINATION"

Anyone who has read the Old Testament knows that prophets frequently told the future. And the Old Testament "prophetic" function carried forward into the New Testament era. Agabus in Acts 11. 27-28 prophesied there would be a great famine throughout the world. He prophesied again in Acts 21. 10-11, foretelling the Apostle Paul's arrest in Jerusalem and his delivery into the hands of the Gentiles.

The issue regarding divination or mediums has always been about the source. If God told the future to His prophets, then the prophet, acting as a "medium" of God's word, was true. If a prophet tried to foretell the future on his/her own, the divination was false.

We see this time and time again in the book of Acts. What is the source of a person's power? And what is the purpose and motivation of a person using that power?

"DIVINATION" (FUTURE-TELLING) FOR TODAY

The question that must be asked is: "Is divination (future-telling/prophecy) to be practiced today? And if not, why not?

Our answer to this question is "Yes." It is one of the spiritual "power gifts" that we will define in Chapter Eleven. But there are some who would say, "No, it should not be practiced today." We think it is necessary to understand the reasoning of those who would negate this powerful and useful practice for us today and why we disagree.

An online article entitled *The Dangers of Divination*[4] is representative of a significant portion of those who hold that prophecy is no longer a viable function today. Here's the main point of their argument:

- Jesus gave the full and final revelation. There is no more "revelation" to be given. Therefore, the role of the prophet [predicting the future] no longer exists.
- Using prophetic techniques to learn secret information or the future is *poisonous*.
- People can be beguiled by spirit-beings who have practiced the art of deception "for thousands of years." Therefore, if we close the door to the use of any power-gifts, we cannot be deceived by spirits through prophetic divination.
- The spirit world is "hidden" from our eyes and information about it cannot be gained by "normal means" of learning.

The problem with this viewpoint is that there is nothing, especially in the writings of the New Testament, to indicate that future-telling ceased. For instance, Agabus prophesied twice in the book of Acts. And Agabus was part of a group that traveled from place to place, all functioning as prophets. They predicted a severe famine would engulf the Roman empire during the reign of Claudius. As a result of their prophetic word, members of the Antioch community sent food-relief to the Christian community in Judea (Acts 11. 29).

Then again, if foretelling the future (divination) went out of use, why did the Apostle Paul exhort, "Do not despise prophecies. Test all things; hold fast what is good" (1 Thess. 5. 20-21)? The Corinthian church was told, "Let two or three prophets speak, and let the others judge" (1 Cor. 14. 29).

IS LEARNING ABOUT THE SPIRIT REALM OCCULT?

The last point the article makes concerns whether learning about the spirit realm is "normal" or "hidden" and what is referred to as "occult." Our experience has been that nothing is "hidden." Down through the centuries, people have had powerful and positive spiritual experiences with the spirit realm, but have learned not to talk about them. Perhaps you are one of them.

A woman whom we encountered in a shamanic workshop shared how she, as a teenager, saw spirits walking around. When she shared this with her pastor, he told her it was demonic. When she persisted and asked her youth pastor for advice, he told her to quit the practice, which she did. Now she regrets having followed their advice because, at an older age, it has been difficult for her to return to the use of her spiritual gift of seeing and to her naturally gifted perception of the spirit realm. The problem is, this woman is not alone. There are many people who find themselves in a similar situation. They stopped using their spiritual gifts because family, friends, or their religious leaders labeled their experiences as "dark" and either forbade it or pressured them to quit.

Our view is that perhaps there would be no "occult" if people were taught how to use their spiritual senses and spiritual gifts. Then things would be less "hidden" and would constitute "normal" learning in our society and churches. What if we assembled groups of seekers to talk about their "spirit experiences" and to learn from each other? How powerful and freeing would that be?

We believe the critical issue for many is that they feel disempowered. People know there is more to be experienced because they have periodic spiritual experiences that tell them so. But if they don't receive the support they need to develop their spirituality, then their spiritual gifts and senses remain turned off and locked away in a box. One thing we know for sure: people of all spiritual and faith perspectives want more than this. They know there is more to experience.[5]

WHAT ABOUT SHAMANIC DIVINATION?

What kind of "divination" do Shamans engage in: fortune-telling or future-telling? The latter. In fact, the Foundation for Shamanic Studies[6] warns their students not to engage in fortune-telling as part of their Foundation education or shamanic practice. So, how do Shamans future-tell?

When Shamans journey, they shift out of ordinary clock-time and move into a non-ordinary sacred dimension where "time" does not exist. Relativity, a physical theory for which there are many proofs, states that there is no such thing as absolute time as an independent aspect of objective reality. Rather, spacetime is relative. Therefore, we think it is reasonable to hypothesize that time does not operate as we know it in the spirit world. That's why when Shamans journey into the non-ordinary realm, they see the past, present, and future all at the same time.

Shamans "see" the future in order to envision what their client will look like healed. It is one of the ways healing occurs. Their purpose is not to "fortune-tell" but rather to "future-tell," "dreaming" a new reality in which their client is healed. Let's take a look at how we think this might occur from a quantum perspective.

A number of mathematical theories have been developed to explain the complexity of the quantum system. What scientists do agree on is that multiple possibilities exist simultaneously (what is called "superposition") until one is at last "observed" or selected. So can our human observations affect a human-scale quantum system? We believe they can.

When a Shaman journeys and sees the past, present, and future all at the same time, they see a number of quantum wave-potentials. And, according to our understanding, the Shaman is able, through intention, to "observe" the wave-potentials and select one. That is why it only takes a "mustard seed of faith" to move a mountain. The intention seizes a possibility that is already there.

Does this sound occult to you? Or is it that we are finally, through science, catching up to the powerful potential that Shamans have been working with for centuries and learning how they conduct their art? Shamanic divination, therefore, is not fortune-telling. It is a wonderful, powerful, and compassionate way of envisioning someone's healing. And if a Shaman seeks to heal people out of compassion, we believe he or she is connected to the right source. Why not accept what Shamans have to offer as insightful, helpful, and beneficial if we've tested their spirits and confirm they are in service to Creator? They can teach us a great deal about healing and interacting with the spirit world.

MAGIC, SORCERY, WITCHCRAFT, SOOTHSAYING (FORTUNE-TELLING), AND NECROMANCY

We now know that Shamanic divination is not associated with fortune-telling. But what about magic, sorcery, fortune-telling, witchcraft, and necromancy? Is Shamanism associated with any of these? The answer is no.

Necromancy. Shamanism may seem to parallel the practice of necromancy. There are people who have passed and moved to the Upper World. Is it possible for a Shaman to travel to the Upper World and communicate with people who have passed over? The answer is "Yes." But for what purpose?

In our shamanic practice, we have visited with people who have passed to the afterlife in the Upper World. We believe, however, that we have had a specific and beneficial reason for visiting those who have passed: to check on a deceased's welfare; to resolve an issue with a person who has passed for the sake of a family member, relative, or friend; or to make sure a person has moved on to the afterlife/Upper World and is not stuck in the Middle World.

"Necromancy," in our opinion, is different from our practice as described above. Necromancy is defined as the practice of magic involving communication with the dead—either by summoning their spirits as apparitions, visions, or raising them bodily—for the purpose of divination, imparting the means to foretell future events, discover hidden knowledge, to bring someone back from the dead, or to use the dead as a weapon.[7]

Necromancers seems to engage in different practices than what shamanic practitioners are involved in. For instance we, as shamanic practitioners, do not perform magic, divination for the purposes of fortune-telling, bringing back the dead in a séance, gathering dark (occultic) information, or using the dead to curse someone. These practices run so contrary to Shamanism that we simply say, there is no similarity whatsoever.

Now that we have shown you how the use of helping spirits and shamanic divination can empower healing, we move into the application of shamanic tools and practices. If you have read this far, bravo to you. You have an open mind, are seeking a deeper level of spirituality, and are eager to move ahead without fear in your understanding of Shamanism.

May the work of my hands (Neh. 6. 16) and the intentions of my heart
(Ps. 19. 14) be pleasing to you, O Lord.

PART II
DIPPING YOUR FEET INTO SHAMANIC
WATERS

You may recall in Part One we talked about walking beside a body of water (ocean or lake) and diving below the surface into a fresh, new and different underwater reality and experience. We compared that to "diving" into a new type of knowledge—Shamanism. Well, let's continue with that analogy.

Let's say that you have really taken to snorkeling. But now you want to learn to be a certified diver, with air tanks, so you can stay under water longer, extend your experience, and maybe even take photographs! That is what Part Two is about; it is all about hands-on learning. We want to help you increase and deepen your understanding of how you can incorporate shamanic tools and practices into your life. We have a whole lot to share with you on this topic!

In Part Two we will teach you how to make practical application of what you've learned above. Obviously, we cannot teach you everything from just reading this book because learning to use shamanic tools and spiritual power gifts requires training and experience. Therefore, if you find you have more interest, we will direct you to our contact information at the end of the book.

In Part Two, we will offer you the following rich content:

- How you can open up to your God-given, natural ability to intuit and perceive, which you need in order to access the spirit world.
- How to protect yourself—an essential practice as you begin to transact with the spirit realm.
- Reference to some basic shamanic tools so that you can start building your own shamanic tool chest.
- A walk through some of the spiritual power gifts that are available to everyone. Chances are, you are already using some of these without being aware.
- Definitions of some advanced shamanic practices. While these techniques require hands-on training, we mention them to make you aware of various kinds of protocols that Shamans conduct.
- And to close our lessons, we will address the possible and powerful reality of integrating the spiritual power gifts with shamanic tools to generate a powerful healing presence.

Before moving on, we need to quickly address a topic that could potentially sabotage some of our reader's interest in venturing into spirit-work. While the Virkler quote below is directed to people in the Christian Church, it pertains to all people who live in a Westernized culture that bases its thinking solely on rationalism. Rationalism tends to inhibit participation in S/spirit-awareness.[1]

If our readers are going to benefit from this book, they must allow their thinking to expand to include such things as intuition, spiritual sensing, spirit-awareness, altered states of consciousness—realities and experiences outside the scope of rationalism.

Authors Mark and Patti Virkler write:

"Spirit-to-Spirit encounters with God have become much too rare among Western Christians. Since rationalism has taken over the Western world in the past few hundred years, the Church has also come under its influence and has not given the attention it should have to the work of the Spirit in our lives."

"Forty-nine percent of the New Testament contains references to spiritual (nonrational) experiences. To be bound by rationalism will effectively cut off half of New Testament Christianity. If one is not relating intuitively to God, but only rationally, he will lose his opportunity to flow in the nine gifts of the Holy Spirit (word of wisdom, word of knowledge, faith, healing, miracles, prophecy, distinguishing of spirits, kinds of tongues and interpretations of tongues); to receive guidance through dreams and visions; to have a fully meaningful and effective prayer life; to commune with the Lord in a dialogue, building an extremely intimate relationship with Him; and to fully experience the inward benefits of true worship."[2]

The difficulty with rationalism is not just a concern for the Christian Church; it is a concern for everyone. The issue isn't with using our rational processes. No one could understand this book if they did not do so rationally. The problem is that our culture has locked itself into a "rational-only" box that prohibits us from trusting any experience that the rational mind cannot grasp. This would include the use of intuition or spiritual perception, how to move in the power gifts, how to use various shamanic tools, or how to journey and interact with helping spirits. All of these require that a person navigate their experience in a nonrational, intuitive, and inspirational mode.

We are not advocating throwing our minds away. Rather, we must consider using more than our mind and intellect to transact our faith and spiritual experiences. We encourage people to balance their mind/intellect with the experiential,

S/spirit-side of living. We address the aspect of intuitional living in the next chapter.

8

OPENING TO MYSTERY THROUGH INTUITIVE LISTENING: TURNING ON OUR SPIRITUAL SENSES

Mystery brings the unknown to our doorstep. What is mystery as it relates to our spirituality? It is something that occurs for which there is no rational explanation except through the power of the Spirit's work. There are many mysteries in the Bible which don't fit into our rational box of reason, such as Jesus turning water into wine, the woman who was immediately healed simply by touching the hem of Jesus' garment, and the power of Moses' staff, which turned into a snake and later drove the great waters of the Red Sea apart. Even if we do not understand everything about how Spirit works, we can join with Spirit's purposes by opening our hearts and minds to that process.

Opening and listening to Spirit is a new frontier for many. The key which unlocks mystery's door is learning to access and listen to our own intuition, the gateway to experience the spirit realm. While you may not think of it this way, we see intuition as a spiritual sense. Jesus' expectation was that we use our spiritual sense of intuition in order to move in unity with the Holy Spirit and helping spirits.

Review our introduction to spiritual senses in Chapter 6 (seeing as perceiving and hearing as understanding). We are

adding to our Chapter 6 definition of spiritual senses by teaching
you about intuition (an expanded version of seeing as perceiving)
and listening (practicing awareness as hearing and
understanding).

So, what exactly is intuition? We describe it as a perception,
as spiritual radar, "gut instinct," or a sense of knowing. It is the
ability to look within ourselves and see, hear, or discern the
messages we are given so that we can become aware of a new and
different reality.

Just as our fingerprints and ears are like a unique signature to
our body, our spiritual sense of intuition is distinctive to each of
us. For example, some people "see" energy or spirits; some
people hear inaudible sounds such as music or someone speaking; others smell nonphysical fragrances or odors such as roses or
cigarettes; and some people "just know" things that they have
never had access to. A person may have multiple methods of
exercising their intuition. Whatever the manner in which you
perceive, intuition is a mechanism by which you can open up to
the spirit realm and receive its messages.

You may have had experiences like some of the ones we've
mentioned above. And as a result, perhaps you have concluded
there is something "strange" or "odd" about yourself. Perhaps
your friends or family have noticed your use of intuition and
labeled you as "weird." Well, you are not! In fact, your intuitional
capacities are something you should celebrate and begin to build
on! They are God-given talents that many others have, just like
you. So get out there and find those people! Begin to connect
with others who are gifted like you so that together, all of you
will be inspired to grow in your talents! No fear!!

WALKING IN THE PHYSICAL AND SPIRITUAL
REALMS AT THE SAME TIME

Interacting in the spirit realm requires not only our ability to
listen or intuit but to believe what our senses are telling us. In

the physical world, many choose to believe only what they can see and explain. But in the spiritual realm, we can choose to believe in the unexplainable, the mystery. In either case, do we have to make a choice between the physical world or the spirit realm? No.

Jesus was able to operate in the physical and spiritual realms at the same time. Remember in Mark 5:24-34 where Jesus was in tune with Himself so completely that He felt "power had gone out from Him?" Physically, He was walking through crowds of people who were pressing in around Him. But spiritually, He became instantly aware that something outside of Himself had drawn out a bit of His energy. He realized the contact was not only with the physical hem of His garment, but with Himself, His essence, His energy. Both Jesus' physical and spiritual senses were engaged at the same time.

This event, an example of living with one foot in the physical world and one foot in the spirit world, is a good way to describe the process of being effective in our shamanic work. We must be aware and living in our physical world, while at the same time being open to perceive the arrival of S/spirit's messages from the spirit world. This is what spiritual listening and intuition are all about!

Renowned theoretical physicist Fred Alan Wolf put it this way:

". . . we in the West are now faced with two basic problems. The first problem is our failure to believe in any worlds of experience outside of what we call reality. The first step in rekindling our lost senses is believing they exist. *You can't see what you don't believe is real.* Once you believe that your lost senses still exist, you need to become aware of them and learn to develop them.

The second is that because we fail to believe in the imaginal realm, we also fail to recognize information from it when it appears to us. ...We must learn to pay attention to that which we normally may not even believe exists..."[1] *We will see it when we believe it. In some sense, each of us "creates" the reality we see out there from our beliefs."*[2]

Summing up what Wolf says, we have to "believe" that spirit-reality exists even if we have not experienced it. And then we have to listen for and intuit it if we are going to experience it. And once we believe, listen and intuit in order to experience the spirit realm, then we can begin to move in the same Spirit-empowered lifestyle that Jesus exhibited and wanted us to live.

Here's another way of talking about turning on your own spiritual senses of listening and intuition. It is like walking into a dark room and making a conscious choice to flip on the light switch. We believe that "seeing in the dark" is a way to describe the spiritual power gifts, which we will explore in a subsequent chapter. The gifts of discernment, words of knowledge and wisdom, prophecy as visions and dreams, and faith come to mind. These gifts originate with Spirit and are made known through intuition and spiritual listening and seeing.

Once you accept that you can "see" what is beyond the rational and explainable, you are heading in the direction of sensing Spirit. Then you can be confident that if you enter a dark room, you won't need to flip on the light switch at all. You can "flip on" your intuition and "see" in the darkness because you have trained yourself to be a good listener of your intuition.

If you are going to train yourself to be an intuitive listener, a good place to start is to:

- Trust your intuition, the inner voice which allows you to hear the quiet direction and wisdom of God.
- "Switch on" the inner self and pay attention to what is illuminated.
- Choose to open your heart to receive wisdom. Wisdom can come from Spirit, helping spirits, trustworthy friends and other sources. By combining

your heart energy with your "third eye" energy, you add power to your experience in receiving wisdom. While the heart sets an intention (purpose, aim, or target) and sends energy out to seek and explore, you can utilize your "third eye" to see/visualize/imagine what you are experiencing.[3]

WAYS TO TRAIN THE MIND TO SLOW DOWN IN ORDER TO LISTEN/INTUIT

While the mind is like a computer which gathers and processes rational information, constant mental evaluation and processing inhibits the effectiveness of our spiritual work. This may seem like an odd statement to make but it is true. It is like hearing static instead of beautiful music on the radio. The shamanic mind must be slowed to allow heart energies to be heard clearly. It is then we are able to effortlessly flow into sacred spirit-space.

There are a number of methods that you can use to train your mind to slow down.

- Listen to soft, instrumental music that floats you into a relaxed (not sleep) zone.
- Repeat a mantra or a Bible verse while deeply and slowly breathing.
- Play a Tibetan singing bowl, said to resonate with the Om, the frequency of the universe.
- Focus on a picture and/or a Bible verse and thoughtfully move through the picture or verse to the spiritual reality behind it. This serves to increase the heart experience.
- Drum or flute to send out your voice and intention into the universe. You can ride that voice and intention into sacred space. Any instrument you play can accomplish this.

- Meditate in order to quiet your body, mind, and heart so you can move effortlessly into the Void.

What, you ask, is the "Void"? It is a place where everything exists and yet nothing exists. It is a place of infinite possibilities, of creativity, of inspiration and tremendous peace. It contains both the known and unknown. It does not conform to "clock time," which is the way we identify movement in spacetime, because there is no time in the Void as we experience it in the physical world. It is a sacred, non-ordinary place. In that space we can receive instruction, gain revelation, explore the source of something, learn about ourselves or others, and bring healing.

With all these methods, we can enter a state of deep, peaceful stillness. We release our thoughts and concerns that are focused on things in the rational mind (like a doctor's appointment that afternoon). We breathe deeply and give ourselves over to allow ourselves to trust the Spirit we encounter, in the place where we are beginning to receive the information we seek.

If you are beginning to train yourself in listening, remember that it is a skill which takes time to learn. With repeated effort, you will experience an ease and success in your abilities.

THE IMPORTANCE OF SELF-CONFIDENCE

An important component of excellent listening is to know yourself well enough: the boundary between who you are and where something or someone else begins. Since all of us live life on the basis of our beliefs, do you know what you believe in? Do you feel confident to act on those beliefs? The pathway to finding your place of power in this life is to know yourself well. Having a strong foundation of self-confidence in the uniqueness of your beliefs is essential in utilizing Shamanic tools.

Ask yourself, "Do I really believe what I say or have I inadvertently fallen into the trap of following the consensus of a particular group?" "Group think," also known as "morphogenic resonance," affects us all. It is turning our beliefs over to what a group thinks, allowing church, friends, family or whatever group we identify with to define what we believe. Sometimes this is done subconsciously and we are not even aware of it.

Needless to say, it is important to understand the extent to which any group has influenced you on an energetic level. You can imagine that this becomes a huge issue if a group's teaching or doctrine informs you that it is not necessary to use your intuition and spiritual senses, which runs completely contrary to the teachings of Jesus.

So are you confident in what you believe? Or are you confident in what others have told you to believe? The truth is that if you give yourself over to others rather than developing your own beliefs, you betray your God-given gift of uniqueness. You also devalue your self-esteem. Doesn't everyone want to think they are unique and precious? In our dealings with people, we have found that one hundred percent do! If you choose to hand yourself and your power over to others, you will find yourself lost, confused and ineffective. Power is inspired by your convictions and how you act upon those beliefs. So then, to summarize, you must know who you are, what you believe, and who you are not, so you can perceive S/spirit more clearly.

MAKING SURE YOUR LISTENING IS CLEAN AND CLEAR

In order to enter what we define as the Void or the S/spirit realm and be able to sense S/spirit, you must be able to listen/intuit in a clean and clear way. There are several ways to do this to make sure your energy is strong and balanced.

- First, you must release preconceived ideas, opinions, outcomes, and judgments of what the spirit realm entails. If you are going to move into non-ordinary/sacred experiences, the self-centered ego has to be parked temporarily and the heart must be allowed to sense and be in charge.

- Second, you need to put aside any fear of being led off-track. Fear is often based on an adherence to logic and conditioning rather than trusting S/spirit. Fear may also be involved in your concern about believing something different than the teaching of a group to which you belong.

- Third, clean yourself of negative energies that affect not only your body but your mind, heart, emotions, and thoughts. Seek out a practitioner who utilizes various protocols for balancing and cleansing your body's energies. Or use sage, essential oils, or other natural essences to cleanse the energy inside and outside your body, even around your living space.

- Fourth, cater to a spirit-oriented lifestyle that includes exercise, healthy foods, meditation, prayer, and laughter. Spend time in nature, loving people, enjoying positive people, and enjoying pets. Just as water conducts energy, the foods you eat and substances you drink either assist or compromise the energy you have.

CLEARING YOUR MORPHOGENIC FIELDS

We are immersed in multiple energy fields all at the same time (otherwise known as morphogenic fields).[4] Some are good and some are not so good. Because energy radiates, we are not only affected by our own energy, but by fields of energy that are in the environment, such as people's emotional states. Emotions are powerful forms of energy. They form a collective (a "field") that flows out into the world and affects everyone to some extent.

For instance, we all know how magnetic fields work, the earth's gravitational field, or even about energy waves that make cell phones work. In each case, the effect of the signal, field, or wave of energy extends beyond the material object itself.

People who are inherently sensitive pick up on these morphic fields. But you have to be smart and able to recognize what energy is yours versus what energy is outside yourself that may possibly be hindering you. If you are going to connect with S/spirit, you need to work every day to know what belongs to you and what is coming to you from other people, and then to separate the two. If you cannot make this distinction, you will inherently confuse who you are with energy that is not yours. This mistake will result in you taking on harmful energy that is not your own, or you believing something false about yourself or others that you did not generate.

If you are not aware of the extent to which your spirit is being affected by a negative morphic field of, say, strong negative emotion, you may not realize that what you consider to be a roadblock may not belong to you at all but to something or someone beyond yourself. You may be trying to clean and clear yourself of an emotional state or way of thinking that you did not create in yourself! You then become frustrated with advancement in your spiritual practices. You have to realize that all of life is energy and is interconnected. Not understanding this leads to discounting yourself and the work that the Spirit is doing in you (Jn. 14. 16-17). Self-evaluation is the opportunity to honestly think about what characteristics and beliefs are unique to you emotionally, morally, spiritually, and socially.

We can illustrate our point with this example: Let's say you are peacefully driving in your car, minding your own business, when someone races by and cuts you off while giving you their "salute finger." If you know who you are and what you believe, you need not waste your emotional energy response on that angry driver's rude behavior. By self-evaluation, you don't have to entangle yourself in the other driver's negative energy.

When you begin to differentiate energies, you gain self-control and are empowered to utilize the strengths and wisdom you've been given. You are able to stay in your own lane, so to speak. Self-evaluation is a key preparation to clear and clean yourself for good listening and intuition. No matter what we do or what we believe, we can all benefit from self-evaluation, because it makes us more effective in our work.

If you are going to consider undertaking a shamanic practice sometime in the future, you can begin the discipline of self-evaluation now. Just remember that, no matter what your issues are, personal or derived from a morphogenic field, you can carry them into the Void, and in the Void ask for help to eliminate any obstacles that may encumber you. Consider making self-evaluation a part of your daily meditation practice.

FUN EXERCISES TO DEVELOP INTUITION

If you think it's a burden or a lifetime task to develop intuition and listening skills, we have some fun exercises you might consider.

Try driving and using your intuition to "sense" what a driver is going to do before they do it. Just make sure you don't close your eyes while you are driving! Or, here's another exercise. Do a little people-watching. Get a sense of what people are feeling, but not from their body language. Try to "pick up" their emotional state. This is always a fun thing to do when you are in an airport waiting for a flight. But be mindful of separating your own emotions from what you may pick up on from others.

Another exercise includes spending time outdoors. But there's a catch. Try sensing what the trees are feeling, or what an animal you see might be thinking or feeling, or what the wind or a mountain might be telling you. You have to really quiet yourself to make this happen.

The last exercise we offer you is to hang out with people who can support your development and encourage you. Share your intuitive adventures with them. Then you can learn that it's okay to fail because no one gets things right all the time.

We're glad we could get you moving in this "intuition/Spirit" direction. And if you are moving that way already, we hope this chapter has given you some good ideas of how to move further along that path.

And just to let you know, all of us at some time have doubts about the truth of what we are hearing. That will pass someday as you become more confident in yourself. Just remember that we come to trust our intuition and listening by keeping a clean body and clear conscience, by testing the spirits, seeking wisdom, trusting our friends, keeping to a quieter regimen of meditation, and trusting ourselves.

✧ 9 ✧
SPIRITUAL PROTECTION:
HOW TO PROTECT YOURSELF

J esus said, "You are the light of the world. Let your light so shine before men, that they may see your good works and glorify your Father in heaven" (Mt. 5. 14, 16). When we commit to living a life of love and goodness, we become "light-bearers," people who literally channel Creator's light. As we go about the work of helping and healing, our light radiates to others as well as to the world around us. But when we open ourselves up to this kind of work, we must put some measures in place to protect ourselves from spirits that can become attracted to our light or that may not have our best interest at heart.

PAUL'S CONCEPT OF SPIRITUAL PROTECTION

The Apostle Paul spoke to this issue of self-protection when he said:

"Finally brethren, be strong in the Lord and in the power of His might. Put on the whole armor of God, that you may be able to stand against the schemes of the devil." "Stand therefore, having girded your waist with truth, having put on the breast-plate of righteousness, and having shod your feet with the gospel of peace; above all, taking the shield of faith with which you will be able to quench all the fiery darts of the wicked one. And take the helmet of salvation, and the sword of the Spirit, which is the word of God" (Eph. 6. 10-11, 14-17).

In the Ephesians quote above, the Apostle Paul's admonition to protect ourselves becomes apparent because there are spirits that promote good and spirits that promote harm. You might be asking yourself, "Does my being a light-bearer automatically call attention to myself because I am doing good?" Yes and no. It is true that the more powerfully and effectively you work in the spirit realm, the more the powers of darkness will recognize you. For while your goal is to bring people freedom in their life, the goal of the powers of darkness is to keep people in bondage to things like addictions and self-gratification.

After reading the Apostle Paul's verses above and what we've just said about gaining more notoriety in the spirit realm, you might become apprehensive. But if the Apostle Paul was overly concerned about the powers of darkness, he never would have told us how to protect ourselves. He would have said, "Run for your life!"—which he didn't. What we would like for you, however, is to be wise and cautious and to learn how to protect yourself.

Paul's idea of putting on spiritual armor probably came from watching a Roman soldier go through the process of putting on his battle gear:

"First, the belt. Next, the breastplate, back and front. Now tie on the shoes. Grab the shield. Put on the helmet. And don't forget the sword."

Translating this to the spirit world, it means for each of us to cover the vulnerable parts of ourselves with defensive or offensive gear. And for us to wear it well! There is no doubt Paul saw his fellow church members in battle gear, going out on forays to fight the forces of darkness. Otherwise, why bother with all the armament? Another way of saying this is, "Don't forget to keep up your guard."

OTHER METHODS OF SPIRITUAL PROTECTION AND CLEANSING

If you find yourself praying for a person's healing or a release from an addiction; if you find yourself moving out into the Void on a consistent basis; if you find yourself using spiritual power gifts (discussed later)—these all bring you closer to the veil that separates the ordinary world from the spirit realm. When you are finished with these activities, there are many ways to cleanse yourself of any unwanted energy that may have followed you back into the ordinary realm. One way is to visualize yourself walking through a waterfall of sacred cleansing water. Another way is to imagine the Holy Spirit washing over you with golden light. You also can sage yourself clean. Or, light a candle and try visualizing its flame purifying your body and your spirit.

In summary, this chapter is our way of reminding you that the more you get involved with healing and spirit work, the brighter your light will become. Working shamanically or in a ministry, you may move unintentionally into areas where some darker forces may not be too excited to have you around. Don't pull back out of fear; that was never Paul's intent. Be smart and use the armor or resources you have to protect yourself.

10

SHAMANIC TOOLS

S hamans use tools that may seem strange or out of sync with our culture and some religious beliefs. After all, what possible benefit could come from a person using sage, feathers, a stone, or a drum? We believe, however, that as you deepen your own process of connecting to S/spirit, you too will come to realize the beautiful simplicity of these tools. They offer incredible power and possibilities for your personal life and for healing; they help you resonate with S/spirit.

Our goal in this chapter is to introduce you to a few shamanic tools we think you might be able to try, some of which you may be working with already. We offer them as introductory knowledge. For instance, some of you may have a meditation practice. Since meditation can be construed as a form of journeying (an essential shamanic practice), you may be surprised to find that you are already performing a version of a shamanic function. Or let's say you like to collect rocks. Some Shamans use rocks for various ceremonies, depending on the rock's energetic qualities. So again, without prior knowledge, you are participating somewhat in a shamanic practice.

In other words, while many of the more extensive practices of Shamanism require training, you already may be dabbling in

Shamanism without even realizing it, and you may be connecting with the spirit realm. Just remember, however, that though the shamanic tools we offer may seem simple, they are quite powerful at affecting movement in the spirit realm, so don't underestimate them. But on the other hand, don't be afraid of them either!

In a later chapter on shamanic practices, we will define some very powerful methods that should only be learned in a supervised setting. They are quite involved and usually require a great deal of explanation and trial. If you think that shamanic "tool use" will stretch your understanding of the spirit world, know that "shamanic practices" will accomplish this many times over. So it's better to pick practices up in a workshop or some kind of training. Contact information for workshops on more shamanic tools and practices is provided at the end of this book. For right now, let us introduce you to a few tools which will gently put you in touch with the spirit realm.

MEDITATION, A FORM OF JOURNEYING

For a Shaman, journeying is an activity that distinguishes them from other alternative, spirit-involved practices such as Wicca, Reiki, or Native American traditions. Since journeying is connected with many complex shamanic functions, we suggest that you use meditation as a simpler and easier vehicle until you can be trained in the shamanic function of journeying.

If you are not familiar with meditation, it starts with finding a quiet place undisturbed by intrusions. Sit on a comfortable cushion chair and close your eyes partially or fully. Speak to the Creator, to the Spirit, and to any spirit helpers you've previously identified. Come into their presence in quiet reverence, offering an open heart and mind to hear what they have to tell you. Meditation is a quiet place where you can receive strong and nourishing peace, as well as allow your intuition and listening skills to blossom.

As you begin to relax, take some deep breaths, breathing in slowly through your nose and out slowly through pursed lips. Breathing in this manner keeps oxygen in the lungs for a longer period of time and actually tells the nervous system that the body is safe and can relax. It is like pushing a "reset button," giving you a fresh start in a different mode of operation.

As you begin this time of quiet listening, remember it is a skill that takes practice. Set a timer for seven minutes. If you can sit quietly that long, we say "Congratulations!" Allow yourself to evolve and grow, knowing that you will be better able to sit and concentrate longer in the days ahead.

Move your consciousness from your head to your heart and expand your awareness outward into what is called the Void. By quieting yourself and listening to the still small voice of the Spirit, you will slowly develop your listening ability that we talked about in the Intuition chapter. Putting on some quiet, gentle music may be of help.

When you journey into the Void, you never know what is going to happen. You never know who you are going to meet or what you are going to see that will give you direction, information, answers to your queries. Go confidently, trusting that the Great Spirit who knows all will relay what you need. Meditation is a great way of quietly moving into the spirit realm without a great amount of training. You can investigate various meditation techniques on the internet.

POWER ANIMALS: USING THE ANIMAL YOU ALREADY HAVE

We want to say something about power animals as a tool, because some people, at some time in their past, became associated with an animal through an experience, dream, or vision. And that animal may have become something akin to a companion or protector over the years.

It is a regular occurrence when we inform a client that we

think they would be better served if we could empower them with a power animal (otherwise known as a helping spirit or ally) to respond, "Oh, is that like the wolf who visits me?" or "Yes, I had an eagle I encountered a long time ago and it has stayed with me over the years."

If you have a particular attachment to an animal—and it doesn't have to be a real one!—it can be a mental visualization or a spiritual connection—you already have access to a wonderful shamanic tool. Call on it, ask it for advice, request its presence, and invite it into your meditation space. Keep your eyes open for another animal that might want to adopt and help you. The spirit-universe has a wonderful way of giving us the power-entities we need to help us live a successful and fulfilled life. When animals show up in unexpected ways, it is not by coincidence. We suggest that you pay attention.

TIBETAN SINGING BOWLS

Have you ever played a Tibetan singing bowl? There's a bit of a technique to them, but it doesn't take long to make them "sing." Such a wonderful, long-lasting resonance, they seem to connect our heart with the universe. There are bowls which oscillate at 417 Hz, a vibration which some claim is beneficial for removing negative energy and for healing. Larger Tibetan bowls vibrate at 528 Hz and are used for calming and healing.

Tibetan bowls are not in every Shaman's repertoire of tools, but we have one in ours. Whatever size you use, try using one during your meditation practice, especially at the beginning. As you begin your meditation time with breathing, also consider using a Tibetan bowl to deepen your state of connection to the sacred, non-ordinary universe. Scientists have shown that alpha and theta waves, which are the slowest neural cycles, result in deep relaxation and activate the subconscious. [1] A Tibetan bowl can help to generate those neural cycles and enhance the quality of your meditation experience.

DRUMMING

By far, the drum is one of the most powerful tools a Shaman uses. Shamans typically use a hoop drum, the skin of which is made of elk, goat, buffalo, horse, or cow. Drums are single or double-sided, most being single-sided. They are usually 14" to 16" in diameter, unless larger for ceremonial purposes. There are also synthetic drums which are much less expensive and not subject to weather changes. They carry a clear nice sound.

Our drums fulfill many purposes for us. We drum for an intention (aim), for prayer, and for worship. We drum for the sake of healing our community, state, nation, and world. We drum to ask our Creator, Holy Spirit, and helping spirits for wisdom. We drum, sending out specific prayers for people. We drum at night under the moon's glow, reminding ourselves of the power of the feminine.

When we begin to drum, unless we already have a specific purpose in mind, we ask S/spirit to show us through the drum what the purpose is for our drumming. This may sound strange, but try this: sit quietly and wait for a drum-beat to come to your heart. Listen for it, then begin to slowly and gently replicate it, then with more fervor as led. Ask S/spirit to give the interpretation of the drum-beat you've been given. It's a fascinating process and a sure way to link you to Spirit.

Our friend, Don Daley, shared this personal reflection with us about the importance of drumming:

"What I believe, what I deem important for my life, can be summed up in one simple, twenty-minute drum-beat song. What is it about this drum-beat? Why, time after time, do I come back to this satisfying reality? It is the calming tone of its voice; it lures me to a deeper place ...

"Not a week goes by that I don't pick up one of my fellow drums and play a song that brings to me a sense of Creator. The deep sounds and rhythms of the beat cause my thoughts to

settle and rest in the presence of its voice. Gentle in its vibra-
tions, this is where I dream during the daylight. It is a pleasant
language that is so special to my existence.

"Today when I drum, the beat reminds me of this relationship. I listen and I am satisfied. There are wonderful moments
as gladness pours out from its rhythm and beat. I am moved by
its voice; forward I go, regardless of the day's journey.

"I have played the hoop drum for many purposes. Personally, I have played the drum to bring me into a place of peace.
This is where I can focus my thoughts to get out of my brain
and move into my heart. These warm tones and pleasing
rhythms lead me to adjust my senses and to know what is
important. Thus, looking and hearing Creator's spirit, I lead
with my intent and then lead out with a drum song. Often, Life-
Giver reveals what I may accomplish in the moment.

"Making the connection between my intent and what can
come in my drum experience has altered my life greatly. Over
the years I have seen many miracles, from healings to blessing
the earth into greater health. Drumming has led me into many
new realms of experience with nature and friends. My
heart. Creator. My heart. Creator. My heart beats in an eternal
relationship with Creator!"

OPENING SACRED SPACE

Any time you engage in an act where you are trying to connect
with S/spirit, take a moment and create sacred space. This may
sound mysterious but it is not; it is actually quite simple and
practical. Imagine you want to create a pure bubble around yourself, a clean environment where only the Spirit and your helping
spirits are invited in, and any negative energy that you or a
person with you may have picked up is moved out. You've seen
those movies where they put people in a plastic, oxygen-rich,
pure environment? It's kind of like that, but energetically.

To do this, simply make several wide, sweeping motions with

both hands and arms starting above your head and arcing out in a wide circle around you to your thighs. As you arc, ask the Creator, Christ-Spirit, Life-Giver Spirit, or helping spirits to come and fill the space with their presence. It's a pretty simple process when you think of it. Do this when you start your meditation practice or if you are going to pray for someone's healing. And when you are done, do the opposite. Close the space by sweeping your hands from thigh-level upward to above your head. In the shamanic realm, it is a good practice to close whatever you've opened.

USING A RATTLE

Rattles are used quite often by Shamans for a variety of actions. For instance, we rattle to invite our helping spirits, to seal a decision we've made, or to open and close ceremonies such as a meditation time. You can find rattles in stores or on the internet. They come in various sizes, shapes, colors, and sounds. Choose the rattle that speaks to you. You will know it is "yours" when you hold it in your hand and shake it.

Some Shamans use a rattle to invite their helping spirits to join them. The rattle is like a Tibetan singing bowl or drum that operates at a certain frequency. It sends out a signal to the universe based on our intention. That's why, whether a person uses a drum, rattle, or singing bowl, nothing is really accomplished unless the heart is engaged. As Don said so eloquently, "This is where I can focus my thoughts to get out of my brain and move into my heart."

Use your rattle for whatever you would like: to start a meditation time, to open sacred space, to connect with the spirit realm, after you've prayed for someone's healing, or just to connect with the environment if you are out for a walk. A rattle is one of those cool tools to keep handy!

FEATHERS AND STONES

Not all Shamans use feathers or stones, but we like to use them. Stones have various energetic properties that are useful for drawing out negative energy, protection, as a prism to focus energy, for gathering up loose or varied energies, or simply for putting out some nice, positive energy. Plus, it is fun to read about the spiritual characteristics of the different stones you might encounter and the way you can apply them.

Feathers move energy. Feathers from different birds do different things. We might use a feather or feathers to brush off some negative energy from a person. If the bird soars, we might use that kind of feather to invite wisdom from the sky for a person. If the bird is a raptor, we might ask it to take something away from a person. If the bird is an owl that sees in the dark, we might ask its spirit to help us or our client "see in the dark" (one of the definitions of a Shaman) when needing to come into deeper understanding. Feathers, like stones, have spiritual properties connected to their particular bird. Look a bird up on the internet to discover its spiritual purpose and use its feather for the same.

When you decide to obtain stones or feathers, especially ones found in the environment, keep the one that feels "right" to you. Don't be afraid or too awkward to ask the stone or feather, "Do you want to come home with me? Do you want to help me?" Then wait. You'll receive the answer. Your hand will become tingly or warm. Or you may get a big sense of "Yes" inside. It is the spirit of the stone or feather that is saying "yes" or "no."

TOBACCO OR SAGE

What "tools" a shamanic practitioner uses depends on their training and what tools speak to them. Throughout history, tobacco has been considered a holy plant. It still is very much in use today, whether it is smoked in a pipe, offered in raw form, or rolled into a cigarette and its smoke blown on a person or object for cleansing, blessing, or protection. We use tobacco to thank our helping spirits. Use of any ceremonial item depends on what we set our focus on. We use tobacco for offerings but prefer to burn sage in order to clean, bless, or protect.

If burning tobacco or sage may seem odd to you, think of the practice of burning incense in an orthodox church. And what about the Buddhist tradition of burning incense while meditating? Historically and in religious traditions, incense was used because it symbolized cleansing and sending prayers upward to God or to the higher realms. So burning tobacco or sage isn't quite so strange as it may sound. Burning sage has a wonderful antibacterial cleansing function. Here's how to give burning sage a try:

Some bookstores and health food stores (find this online) sell abalone shells and white sage. Put a little sand in the bottom of the abalone shell to extinguish the sage when you are done. Break off a stem of white sage with the leaves attached. Light it up, then blow it out somewhat quickly so that you only have smoking embers. Now, use your hand or a feather and fan the smoke over yourself. Imagine you are cleaning yourself off; use the smoking sage to strip away any unwanted energy surrounding you and push it toward the ground. Imagine creating an energetic hole in the floor where the energy you pull off is channeled into the earth for reconstitution. Then use the sage to call blessings in from Creator; the Christ-Spirit; the Life-Giver Spirit; your helping spirits; or elements in the universe.

Sage the person with you, or a spouse, partner, or child. Sage your pets. Then, in your mind's eye, visualize your house and your property. Fan smoke in the direction of the edges of your property and set the intention for the smoke to carry away unwanted energy and spirits. If you need to cleanse your house, fan the smoke into each room and into all the corners with the goal that you are sending any unwanted energy through an energetic hole, into the safekeeping of Mother Earth.

This is called smudging. It is a simple and fantastic way you can cleanse yourself, your spouse, your children, your pets, and your home. You can successfully sage people (and things) even without them being present, but only with their consent, of course.

THE STONE CIRCLE

A stone circle is highly symbolic. It is a space where heaven, earth, the six directions, and our spirits converge. It is a focal point or prism of spirits and power. Circles are very sacred.

Sally built a stone circle in her backyard as a way of creating a sacred space for prayer. It is the place where we worship the Creator, where we seek guidance, the place from which we send blessing to our community, state, nation, and world. We drum in our circle, sending out prayers for people and the land. It is the place where our helping spirits come to commingle with us, to dance, and to enjoy our company—as well as each other's.

Circles are easy to build. You can make them as large or small as you'd like. They can consist of as few as four small rocks to mark the compass directions. However elaborate your circle is, once built, cleanse it with sage, set your intention for its purpose, and keep it as a sacred meeting place for you and your spirit helpers. Traditionally, it is important that, once you set and bless your circle, you always ask permission before you step inside. It is a sign of respect for the sacredness of that space. And it makes us monitor ourselves to determine whether we are in a good mental and heartful place to access Spirit.

CANDLES

Did you think we forgot this most common tool? Candles have been used for generations to bring light to darkness. Besides often having a wonderful scent, candles can be a focal point for gatherings, especially on the table at mealtimes. The fire of the flame brings purification. It is alive, bringing warmth to the cold. It has been said that when the flame extends up long and tall that there are good spirits present!

Being careful not to burn yourself, light the wick, then move your hands behind the candle. Then bring your hands over the top of and across the flame toward your heart, drawing the flame's energy toward you. Repeat moving the flame's energy to you and over your head. This brings the light of life to you, the spirit of fire, for your eyes to see clearly, your mind to open to wisdom, and your ears to hear truth clearly. It can represent burning away what is not needed in your life anymore. We encourage you to create your own prayer intention!

CONNECTING TO THE ENVIRONMENT

There are many reasons why people are disconnected from their natural environment. One of the biggest reasons is that a large majority of people live in cities. Their environmental needs (water, sewage, food, transportation, safety, protection from weather) are all taken care of for them. So, there is no incentive for them to connect with nature and observe its many changes and patterns.

What we are advocating in this section is an awareness of S/spirit, especially in the environment. Shamans believe that all of creation is alive with spirit—the sun, moon, sky, clouds, wind, mountains, trees, shrubs, Earth, animals, insects, reptiles, etc.— everything. As we pay attention to it, we come to find out that the environment is constantly talking to us about itself, about us, about our impact on it, about living simply, efficiently, and in a healthy way.

The next time you are outside, wherever you are, stop and talk to the earth elements. Talk to the air. Without realizing it, when you breathe the air, you are in touch not only with the breath of the Creator, but with the breath of every human being and animal on the planet, everything that is living and that has S/spirit.

Take time to thank the mountains you may be visiting. Look up in the sky and thank the sun for its light and warmth, the moon for its soft feminine energy and wisdom. Thank the clouds for their moisture and the wind for bringing words of wisdom. Thank Mother Earth for reconstituting the energy of our pain and suffering and for her healing. Value the trees who symbolize how we are to live our lives, that is, reaching to the heavens for truth and at the same time setting deep roots down into Mother Earth to replenish our nourishment.

Take a little tobacco and make an offering of gratitude to the earth elements. When you make that offering, the Earth will begin to speak to you because you have taken the time to enter into a relationship with its spirit. And so, quiet your heart and mind to listen to S/spirit like we talked about in the Intuition/Listening chapter (Chapter 8).

Don't forget to say a prayer of worship and thanks to the Creator for this awesome creation. Mention your gratitude and awe because the Creator not only made our beautiful planet, but also the spirits attached to it, who offer their help and energy (chi).

We have offered you a few shamanic "tools" to use. We think you will have fun working with them. And like we said, their use will move you further and further into contact with the sacred, non-ordinary, spirit realm.

Perhaps after using some of these tools and reading our upcoming chapter on Shamanic Practices, your curiosity will lead you to take some hands-on training in Shamanism. If you do, that will be exciting for you. But first, a word of warning.

KEEP IT SIMPLE

A danger for people, once they begin to move further into the practice of Shamanism, is to collect paraphernalia that make people take notice of them, items that say, "Look at me! I'm shamanic." Yet our mentors tell us that when it comes to shamanic dress and paraphernalia: "Keep it simple."

Perhaps the two greatest qualities anyone could exhibit are compassion and humility. This also applies to how people dress and conduct themselves as shamanic practitioners. When we address this topic, we think of Jesus as our model. He was a simply dressed man who spoke directly, touched the sick, and moved in power. He was "connected." That's how we want to be.... the real deal, humbly doing our work. We may drum, flute, use a rattle, burn sage, offer tobacco, or use stones and feathers. But we don't forget that these are all ancillary to the true character of who we are and what we do, which is to set an intention from a pure heart, walk humbly, and manifest compassion for the benefit of others and our environment. This is true Shamanism!

11

SPIRITUAL POWER GIFTS

We have mentioned the phrase, "spiritual power gifts," on multiple occasions. It is time now for us to tell you exactly what we mean by that phrase and bring your attention to what is unique about them.

ALL THE SPIRITUAL GIFTS

Spiritual gifts are listed in a number of locations in the Bible:

- 1 Cor. 12. 8-10, 29: Wisdom, Knowledge, Faith, Healing, Miraculous Powers, Discernment of Spirits, Tongues, Interpretation of Tongues, Helps, Administration, Apostleship, Prophecy, Teaching.
- Rom. 12. 6-8: Prophecy, Teaching, Serving, Encouragement, Exhortation, Giving to Others, Leadership, Mercy.
- Eph. 4. 11-13: Apostleship, Prophecy, Teaching, Pastoring, Evangelism.
- Other possible gifts include: Celibacy, Hospitality, Intercession, Creative Abilities, Missionary Work, Exorcism, Martyrdom, Voluntary Poverty.

104 STEPHEN M. BULL & SALLY H. DENNY

THE POWER GIFTS

Of the gifts which Scripture mentions above, we define some of them as "power gifts." They are called "power gifts" because our human efforts are not enough to activate them. They require the specific empowerment by the Holy, Life-Giver Spirit or by our helping spirits.[1] The "power gifts" are: Word of Wisdom, Word of Knowledge, Faith, Healing, Miracles, Prophecy (Dreams and Visions), Distinguishing (Discernment) of Spirits, Tongues and the Interpretation of Tongues.

Our belief is that Shamans and shamanic practitioners use *most* of the same power gifts: Words of Wisdom, Words of Knowledge, Healing, Miracles, Prophecy (Dreams and Visions), and Discernment of Spirits. As the saying goes, they "drink from the same well," that is, from the same source of the S/spirit. Therefore, in this chapter, it is our goal to define each of the power gifts so that all our readers can understand what is available to them to use in their lives and service.

Some of our other-than-Christian readers might wonder, "If spiritual power gifts have been given in the Bible, shouldn't Christians be experts in the affairs of S/spirit and power?" The answer is "Yes, theoretically." Unfortunately, many Christians know very little about matters of the Spirit. Why is that?

On a local church level, spirit-training falls on the shoulders of the local pastor. The problem is that many pastors have never been trained in the exercise of spiritual gifts themselves. Some ministers have succumbed to the mentality of Western rationalism that refuses to acknowledge the supernatural or the existence of spiritual power gifts. Then again, many are unsure of how to handle manifestations of the Spirit in their congregations. Out of fear, they squelch the movement of the Spirit.

This is the predicament many church members find themselves in today. Pastors pick and choose which gifts are appropriate for their church members to practice and which are not. Typically, the power gifts are considered unacceptable. As a result, many Christians feel forced to go outside their church to be trained in supernatural practices, for which they are often criticized.

You may adhere to Christian beliefs but know very little about power gifts. Or perhaps you do not follow the teachings of Jesus but also don't know much about power gifts. In either case, all of you, our readers, will benefit from this chapter. The use of shamanic tools, coupled with spiritual gifts, will make for a powerful healing practitioner.

LIMITING THE DISCUSSION OF POWER GIFTS FOR THE SAKE OF BREVITY

A presentation on all the power gifts would be quite lengthy. For the sake of brevity, we are limiting our definition of the power gifts to those most commonly used: word of knowledge, word of wisdom, healing, prophecy as dreams and visions, and discernment of spirits. A brief presentation of the other power gifts can be found in the Endnotes.[2] As you read our description of these power gifts, ask yourself which ones you are manifesting, even if in a small way, and how you might develop and increase them.

SPIRITUAL POWER GIFTS

Word of Wisdom

"The supernatural ability to offer pertinent spiritual counsel immediately in situations where such guidance is needed."[3] R. Clinton states that the word of wisdom "represents the capacity to know the mind of the Spirit in a given situation and to communicate clearly the situation, facts, truth, or application of facts and truth to meet the need of the situation."[4]

Our friend Don, who wrote the beautiful piece above on drumming in the Shamanic Tools chapter, operates with Words of Wisdom. When Don speaks, we stop and listen. He has a profound sense of seeing into the depth of situations and interpreting them on a spiritual/spirit basis.

Don says things that we did not think to ask about the different facets of an experience or its meaning. When he finishes speaking, we know we must weigh what he has said.

In a Shamanic or Church ministry situation, start by asking the S/spirit for help. For instance, you might ask: "How do I interpret this situation? How do I deal with this spirit? How can I get a better sense of what's causing this person's pain? How do I start a healing session with this person? How can this person improve their life?" The Spirit or your helping spirits will give you the wisdom you ask for. You don't need to be a shamanic practitioner to ask these kinds of questions.

An idea will come to you from the Great Spirit. Sometimes it will take a few minutes, but if you are patient the answer will come. It may come as a visualization, that is, you see it in your mind's eye. You might sense it, come to have an immediate knowledge of what or how to do something. You may hear an audible word, a single word or short phrase. You may feel something in your body that is also going on in the body of the person with whom you are working, followed by an idea of how to rectify it. In whatever form that wisdom comes, be patient, wait for it. The point is to quiet yourself, dial down, and tune in. The S/spirit never disappoints.

Word of Knowledge

"The supernatural ability to receive and share revealed knowledge which was not otherwise known, or the ability to gather and clarify large quantities of [biblical] knowledge with unusual spiritual insight." [5]

We've mentioned already how Jesus had words of knowledge, that is, He knew things about people without prior knowledge.[6] Rather, He operated with all the gifts of the Spirit.

During our shamanic work, it has become quite common for

us to receive words of knowledge. Having a word of knowledge reveals things to us about a situation or person that we did not know before, such as: how a person is feeling, the cause of their illness, or what they are struggling with.

When the word comes it tends to be simple, direct, and quick. It is important to pay attention and not doubt what is heard. Many times in our work with clients, we have received a Word that does not make sense to us. But when we share it with the person to whom we were ministering they are shocked and say, "Yes, that's very applicable; that's right on the money! Thank you."

So here's our advice: Pay attention to your spiritual senses of listening and seeing and feeling. The more you do so, the more surprised you will be at how much information the S/spirit passes to you quickly, quietly, simply, and directly. Hearing from Spirit applies in any life situation, not just in ministry or shamanic work. And whatever you hear, don't doubt it; believe what the Spirit tells you.

Healing

"The supernatural ability to miraculously restore health to an individual in the physical, emotional, or spiritual realms through the direct act of God."[7]

Healing encompasses many aspects of our lives and our interaction with the world around us. We often speak of healing what is broken in the areas of relationships or illness. Healing puts things back into a state of balance. In illness, there is healing through medicines either with natural or pharmaceutical remedies. In relationships, brokenness is overcome through the power of love, acceptance and forgiveness. As we well know, sometimes the available medical, emotional or spiritual remedies do not work, for whatever reason. Therefore, infusing the power of S/spirit with unique wisdom and insight into a person's brokenness becomes a necessary ingredient for healing. Healing brings peace so that whatever is broken can be made whole.

Jesus was a healer. We learn a great deal about healing by studying His ministry.

- Healing and teaching/preaching were always linked in Jesus' ministry. In other words, it is okay to explain to someone the basis on which you are healing them— where your power comes from.
- Jesus often touched the people whom He healed as a way of connecting with them. Touch should only be done with permission.
- Jesus often gave people whom He healed something to do as part of their healing process. This required the use of their faith, which aids in healing.
- Sometimes people were healed instantly by Jesus, and sometimes their healing was delayed. So don't get down on yourself if someone you prayed for, or did shamanic work on, wasn't immediately healed. Healing occurs in many ways, in its own time, according to the need of each person.
- Jesus had compassion for those whom He healed, always a prerequisite for doing any kind of spiritual work.
- Jesus explained that fear and doubt were the enemies of healing.
- Jesus was always ready to heal people. Sometimes He had to remove a person from a negative environment that was not conducive to their healing.
- Jesus was greatly assisted in His healing by words of knowledge.

Everyone is gifted with the ability to heal (Mk. 16. 17-18). Healing is a sign—of a new age, of the love and power of God advancing in the world. It is the empowerment of all people by the Spirit for the sake of compassionate works of service (Acts 2. 17). Though everyone can heal, there appears to be a specific gift of Healing (1 Cor. 12. 9, 28). Those with this gift seem to work more powerfully in that arena.

Prophecy

"Prophecy is the supernatural ability to proclaim God's present and future truth in such a way that the hearers are moved to respond."[8] The Apostle Peter wrote: "No prophecy of Scripture came about by the prophet's own interpretation. For prophecy never had its origin in the will of man, but men spoke from God as they were carried along by the Holy Spirit" (2 Pet. 1. 20-21).

Any kind of prophecy should call people back into a healthy, balanced relationship with themselves, others, the environment, and their Creator. Prophecy may involve a physical healing, but it often pertains to a larger issue, such as challenging a person to leave an addiction or a harmful lifestyle. It may focus on a concern for social injustice. Prophecy promotes Creator's agenda for health, unity, balance, and rightness.

Jesus' prophetic gifting called him to "set things right for God." For instance, one of the things Jesus is famous for is chasing the money changers and merchants off the Temple grounds. Ex-patriots made yearly pilgrimages to celebrate Jewish feast days, traveling from all over the Mediterranean and Asia Minor to the Temple in Jerusalem. The Temple clergy charged the pilgrims a large fee to change their foreign currency into temple currency and exorbitant rates to purchase an animal to sacrifice. This exploitation of people who came to worship God caused Jesus to shift into a prophetic, zealous mode, fulfilling the prophecy in Ps. 69: "Zeal for Your house [God's house] will consume me."

On another occasion, Jesus challenged the Pharisees (reli-gious-political party) when they accused him, incorrectly, of breaking the Mosaic law by healing on the Sabbath.[9] Jesus said to the Pharisees: "Stop judging by mere appearances and make a right judgment" (Jn. 7. 24). As a prophet, Jesus was calling the theocrats of His day to interpret the law according to Creator's intention, not their own.

Prophecy comes to us through being open to Spirit, actively listening to it. If we are tuned in and Spirit is speaking to us, we will be able to hear the message being communicated. To operate prophetically is to speak truth without fear, calling people to live consistent with Creator's life and purposes. This should be the essence of all prophetic words in whatever form they come. Healing and a prophetic word combine very powerfully together.

Dreams and visions were not a rare occurrence to Old and New Testament characters in the Bible, although in our day and age some think they seem quite rare. According to Acts 2. 17, one of the ways people function prophetically today is through dreams and visions. Dreams and visions are powerful forms of visualizing something that Spirit knows will take place.

Dreams and visions often overlap in terms of their function, but they are different. While someone may "dream" during the day (i.e., daydream), dreams typically occur at night. Visions, on the other hand, can occur day or night.

When we talk about dreams and dreaming in this book, we are not referring to the kinds of dreams people have every night. Rather, we are dealing with dreams that are Spirit-given, in a nontypical, non-ordinary state of consciousness in which the dreamer connects with Creator, Spirit, helping spirits, or what is termed the "supernatural."

Dreams can fulfill a number of spiritual objectives: provide wisdom or insight; direct efforts for healing; show how some kind of upcoming event is going to unfold and how to respond to it; help the dreamer to challenge people about a social or religious/spiritual issue; or introduce the dreamer to a deeper experience within the spirit realm. Here is an example of how a dream can be experienced and its interpretation applied.

Don's "Wave" Dream. You've already met our friend Don in this chapter in reference to the gift of Wisdom, and in the Shamanic Tools chapter about drumming. At this time, we are going to learn about a powerful prophetic dream Don had that took place many years ago. Don didn't realize he was going to have the "mother of all dreams" until, having gone to bed one evening, he awoke 2.5 days later having dreamed the whole time! Now there are dreams, and then there are DREAMS. And this was a DREAM that lasted an entire 2.5 days!

We can learn about dreams and their meaning by "listening in" on Don's dream and its interpretation. Here's the substance of Don's dream as relayed to me (Steve). It is followed by some interpretations offered by Don.

Don found himself aboard a ship, a three-masted sailing vessel like the Mayflower. He was at the helm and directing the ship, with no prior experience! There was a Captain standing behind Don. The Captain was large in stature, wore a blue uniform and cap, had strong facial features and large powerful hands. He showed Don how to steer and navigate the ship. The Captain's commands to Don and the crew were precise, clear, and supportive. The crew performed their duties. Don and the crew felt great contentment when following the Captain's orders.

The weather began to change. A storm was brewing and on its way. Nevertheless, and with the captain's presence and encouragement, Don felt confident and competent.

The ship was sailing well and Don's attention was captured by its construction and details. There were things about the ship that made Don realize this was a dream. For instance, while the ship was very old, it was carrying modern crates labeled for distribution to contemporary cities. There were propane lanterns lighting the below-deck areas. There were people on board, women and children, whom Don previously had not seen and who suddenly appeared. Those people, when the storm came, tried to line the inside of the ship with plastic to keep water out. Odd.

The Captain brought Don's focus back to the storm, a "good storm," the Captain said. The Captain had Don reassure the crew and passengers that everything would be alright, though there was a sense of unknowing.

Eventually the storm broke upon the ship with large, dark grey and green seas, whitecaps, a darkened sky, and a wind that seemed to blow from everywhere, making it impossible to look in any direction. Luckily the crew had rigged the ship for heavy seas. Some of the heavier crates had to be tossed overboard.

The Captain ordered Don to put the ship on a different course, heading toward a small but safe harbor to wait out the storm. Protected, Don and the crew began making repairs, found needed rest, and began the search for food and water.

The next day dawned wonderfully beautiful and tropical until Don noticed something odd. He observed that the line of the horizon was about ten to twenty feet higher. This made no sense to Don and the Captain wasn't around to explain. But the explanation came soon enough in the form of a gigantic tsunami wave that crashed into the ship, lifting it over the island's mountain range and sending it and Don and everyone tumbling head over heels.

Don was washed overboard and pressed down under water into what had been, moments before, a wheat field. Pinned under, Don started running out of air but discovered a brief source of trapped air. However, even this little bit of air quickly gave out. Don called out to God for help and then lapsed into unconsciousness. Time seemed to stop. Then slowly, somehow, Don became aware that light flickered in and filled his body. His senses kicked in to tell him that, even though he couldn't see, he was laying in inches of water. Even though Don was weak and unable to move, he felt protected, though vulnerable.

Too weak to get up, Don waited for the sun to dry things

out. Finally, Don forced himself to sit up and open his eyes.
What he saw astonished him. Stretched out before him was
green grass filling a sweeping valley, a crystal-blue lake
surrounded by majestic purple mountains, and a royal blue sky
framed by billowy clouds. But best of all, he heard worship, a
song sung by people close by that penetrated and strength-
ened his spirit. He felt exhilarated, overwhelmed. Don fell to
his knees, reached to heaven, and wept tears of joy as a
worshipful chorale raised a crescendo of praise. The dream
ends here.[10]

Dreams like Don's keep expanding in meaning over the years.
They can speak directly to the dreamer or to others like us. The
power of dreams lies in the interpretation that S/spirit gives to
the dreamer or to those gifted in prophecy who can explain the
dream's meaning. Don's understanding of his dream follows. His
interpretation is not only for himself but for anyone to whom
the dream speaks.

- The Captain is a symbol of the Christ-Spirit, who
  loves and cares for Don and makes him feel secure.
  The Captain's stature, uniform, strong hands and
  features told Don that the Christ-Spirit has authority,
  is in control, and can be trusted. In fact, our sense of
  competency in life can arise because of our
  connection to the Christ-Spirit who supports us.
- The fact that Don never sailed before represents a
  facet of life he had not yet lived. This new facet
  foretold a future of adventure and the discovery of
  new people and cultures. The dream showed Don that
  he could feel at ease moving into new situations
  because the Christ-Spirit would watch over him like
  the Captain in the dream.
- Don gave orders to an experienced crew. And while
  novel, it showed him that he could self-identify as a

leader or a person with leadership qualities whom
people would be willing to follow.

- There is a tendency for any of us to become focused
on the details of our lives instead of seeing the larger
picture. When the Captain made Don aware of the
approaching storm, he pulled Don out of his reverie
and brought his attention back to the reality at hand.
So keeping an ear open to the Christ-Spirit's leading is
a good practice, as indicated by the dream.

- The Captain described the storm as "good." This
demonstrates the inevitability in life that we will face
hardships, but are not to fret. We should anticipate
that good things can come of "storms" if we are
patient and don't panic or become too depressed.

- When Don encountered some oddities (modern
crates, propane lanterns, and people), he realized that
there was a larger aspect to the dream and what it
would mean to himself and others. Also, there is a
timeless sense to the dream; it could be applied to any
age or epoch.

- The storm was fiercer than expected. Cargo had to be
put overboard. The meaning here is: when the storms
of life hit, do an inventory of your life. Be flexible,
adaptable, and ready to get rid of things that are no
longer useful during the transition. Carry only what
you need. Live simply.

- The Captain instructed Don to change course—Don
the neophyte helmsman! This simply says that we can
improve our life-skills even in the midst of a life
storm.

- The storm slackened, followed by a beautiful, restful
day, until the tsunami arrived. The idea here is that
things can calm down but we shouldn't become
complacent. A rogue incident can upend our lives at
any moment, so let's not be too unprepared. Have

some extra savings on hand, a full tank of gas, and a close connection with the Christ-Spirit.
- The tsunami hit and everything was turned upside-down. Sometimes in these situations, we go through a kind of death-experience. Part of ourselves (or all) gets pressed into a difficult place and we feel like we are losing our life (maybe not physically but certainly emotionally and spiritually). We wonder, "Why is this happening to me?" And we cry out to God.

This is when we experience "mystery," the transition from old to new, from death to new life, from stasis to growth. We become "born again." No one can explain what prompts us to change. But suddenly we agree to the opportunity to change that has come our way. We say "Yes" when we could just as easily say "No."

When the mystery occurs, we are vulnerable. Our eyes, like Don's eyes in the dream, are closed. We feel weak. But if we are patient, the sun (as in Don's dream) comes out. We get up and step into a whole new reality.

And as we experience this new reality, we have something to worship about, something powerful and positive to say about the process. We begin to hear the song of the universe in praise of the Christ-Spirit who, as our Captain, actually has accompanied us through our transition, bringing a miracle of growth our way. A song fills our heart that penetrates our being. We, like Don, are exhilarated and overwhelmed.

This is the power of dreams which can carry us to new meanings and new understandings. Dreams are authored by Spirit and given so we can pass through the mystery to a whole new level of consciousness and development.

Obviously, not all dreams people might have are as powerful as the one Don had. But according to Acts 2, nothing has stopped the Spirit from moving in this powerful way. Therefore, we should expect dreaming like Don's to take place on a fairly regular basis—just not for 2.5 days!

Visions

Regarding visions, Wikipedia explains that a vision is something seen in the imagination or the supernatural based on a mystical or religious experience. It is something "seen," possibly during the day, and not so much with the physical senses as with spiritual sight, hearing, sensing, etc. As a young child, Sally's visioning daughter once said: "Mommy, it is like dreaming with your eyes open."

In the New Testament, there were a number of people who had visions: Stephen, the first Christian to be martyred (Acts. 7); the Apostle Peter in Acts 10; the Apostle Paul in Acts 9, 16, and 18. Seeing visions, one of the power gifts, was nothing new to New Testament life, and visions shouldn't be a strange occurrence to us today. We should expect them. Here are a couple of examples.

Steve's visions. Steve was driving from Oregon to Montana on his way to a vision quest in the Bighorn Mountains where he would receive a life-changing vision experience. While driving, and before he reached his destination, the face of an old "grandmother," a Native American woman, came up in front of him like a heads-up display. She forcefully stated, "Don't doubt!" She repeated this admonition several times. "Okay," he said, "I won't!" She said it again even more forcefully—"Don't doubt!" He knew this extraordinary message was important, even though he didn't know why at the time.

Several days later, Steve engaged in his vision quest, which lasted many days. During that time he had colorful and graphic visions of receiving the help of three very powerful spirit-guides. These allies not only accompanied him on this particular vision quest, but became prominent figures afterwards, significantly influencing his spiritual work.

Why did grandmother spirit come in a vision to Steve? Well, it was during that vision quest that he received healing and direction for some very important decisions. Spirit communicated through the visions and Steve received the knowledge. After having such profound and life-changing experiences, Steve could have doubted what was revealed to him on his vision quest or thought that perhaps those experiences hadn't really happened. However, that is exactly why grandmother had made her special visit—to prepare him not to doubt! Not only has grandmother's voice come back to him on many occasions as a reminder, but he has shared this powerful vision with others and helped them not to doubt what they've received from S/spirit.

Sally's vision. We were aghast following the events in New York City on the morning of September 11, 2001. But not more so than Sally who, the next day, had a very powerful vision. In this particular vision, Sally saw a woman who was trapped and buried amidst rubble in one of the collapsed Twin Tower buildings. The woman was injured and called out for help, but no one heard her pleas. At first Sally thought she was just seeing one of the many victims who was trapped. But the next day, because an internal visual picture of the woman kept returning to her mind's eye brought by the Spirit, Sally realized she needed to pay attention to this particular woman.

Sally became very claustrophobic any time she was inside her house. Seeing this as a sign, Sally went outside and sat down in her backyard. Closing her eyes, Sally went in spirit to be with the woman. The woman was in pain and afraid so Sally decided to hold her hand and stay with her until help arrived. Words of comfort were shared along with stories of the woman's life and family over a four-day period. Because she was trapped so high in the rubble of the collapsed building, no rescuers could have heard her or rescued her, even though Sally kept holding out for hope that it would happen.

Over the next few days, Sally returned often to visit the

woman. She would shift in spirit to be with the lady and then return to "real time" to care for her family's needs.

The day came when physical death came to the woman whose body was still trapped in the rubble, the woman whom Sally had spent time with. Sally helped escort the deceased woman's spirit through the veils of the physical world and into the spirit realm. As confirmation of the validity of what Sally had experienced, several days later pictures of the presumed dead were published in the newspaper. Looking at the images of those who had died, Sally recognized the photo of her friend and had a realization of the serious work she had been called to do.

We've shared only a few of the many powerful visions that have affected our lives. Our guess is that a good number of you may have had similar experiences but kept quiet out of fear of being ridiculed. The fact is, we should no longer be quiet about such occurrences. If anything, we should share them because we continually exude a morphic field with others that creates the power to bring the S/spirit realm more fully into people's consciousness.

Because the Spirit has been poured out on all flesh (Acts 2), we can all dream and have visions. Yet since this is a spiritual (power) gift, the reality is that some people will have more spiritually powerful dreams or visions and with more frequency than others. We definitely need to listen to those who seem to move more powerfully in this gift than the rest of us. So for those who dream and have visions, it's time to speak up so that you can be heard!

Discernment of Spirits

"The supernatural ability to determine whether a certain action has its source in God, man, or Satan."[11] Discernment pertains to distinguishing or differentiating.

Essentially, the role of a person with a gift of discernment is to test (assay, prove, examine) the spirits (1 Jn. 4. 1-3). Testing determines if what a person is saying is given by a good spirit (Phil. 3. 8) or an evil, deceitful spirit (1 Tim. 4. 1).

Discernment comes in handy not only to find out what kind of spirit we might be dealing with, but to determine how it negatively affects the person to whom it is attached. We can use discernment to determine the correlation between the spirit and the condition of the person (physical, emotional, spiritual, etc.).

Here are some tell-tale signs that you are involved with a spirit that is not good:

- The hair on the back of your head stands up.
- You get goosebumps for no reason.
- You start to feel angry without a cause.
- You think something is wrong or about to go wrong and it doesn't.
- The air becomes uncommonly cool or freezing for no reason.
- You feel nauseous or light-headed.
- You develop a strong sense that you shouldn't be doing what you are doing.

Let us assure you that just because you discern the presence of a negative spirit and may experience any of these signs, it does not mean you have to "do" anything about the spirit. You can tell the spirit it is not welcome and that it has to leave "at once!" You can choose not to interact with the spirit unless you have experience or are working with someone who knows what they are doing.

On the other hand, discernment can be used to sense the presence of good, positive spirits. We should test for these as well. Consider asking any spirit that presents to you as an ally, "Who do you serve?" As Bob Dylan sang, "You have to serve somebody. It may be the devil or it may be the Lord, but you have to serve somebody." While Dylan's verse may seem a little tongue-in-cheek, there is truth to it. All spirits serve something or someone higher up the spiritual chain of command.

EXPERIENCE WITH THE POWER GIFTS

These are some of the power gifts. You will probably experience some (like word of knowledge) without realizing it; they will come to you without a great deal of thought or preparation. But there may be times when you ask S/spirit for immediate help with a specific gift. And you will be surprised how quickly it comes.

The last word we want to share with you on this subject is that the use of power gifts fits hand-in-hand with shamanic practices. Consider how you might use a shamanic method for healing along with a word of knowledge or wisdom or discernment of spirits. Create an intention to start moving in these gifts and look for opportunities where you can use them. Expect them to come and they will.

12

ADVANCED SHAMANIC
PRACTICES

When we were first exposed to Shamanism, we had no idea what shamanic practices entailed. We would get bits and pieces of activities from reading books. But it seemed they offered no consistent larger picture that could help us decide whether we wanted to pursue Shamanism or not. We want to spare you that roadblock by using this chapter to define some of the more advanced shamanic practices.

While it is impossible to define all that Shamans do because their practices are so extensive and varied, what follows are some of the more standard practices that Shamans perform. We issue the caveat that, though we define these for you, they are advanced practices and should be undertaken only with training.

JOURNEYING

There is no defined shamanic way to journey. Each journey is new and fresh, never the same. In today's Shamanism, journeying is done by lying down in darkness, or putting on an eye covering to block out the light. A drum or rattle is played with a steady, fast beat, and an intention is set for what the Shaman is trying to accomplish. Then the journeyer's consciousness drifts into an altered state in the Void. The Void can include the Lower, Middle, or Upper worlds. Interactions with S/spirits can occur in any of those dimensions.

Generally, no two persons' journeys are the same. It is possible, however, for two people to journey with the same intention and come to similar conclusions or impressions. This is a powerful validation that the shamanic process works.

For instance, we journeyed for the healing of a person who had cancer. We were given no specifics about their condition, yet after journeying separately, we determined the same location of the cancer in the person's body and actually saw the cancer and the extent of its malignancy. Sometimes, however, our journeys produced different results. The benefit is that we may be led to obtain a broader, more robust view of the person's situation.

Our belief is that the shamanic journey constitutes a major difference between Shamanism and other spirit-oriented modalities such as Wicca or Reiki.

Setting an Intention

Typically, before beginning to journey, the person states their goal for the journey in their own mind several times. It can be helpful to restate the intention during a journey if a person begins to feel like they are not getting anywhere, or if they feel motionless. In all cases, a strong purpose is paramount for a successful journey. If a person does not set a specific intention, their journey will most likely be weak, and the person might wander around the spirit world. Best to avoid that.

Asking for the Aid of Helping Spirits

Once the intention is set, the journeyer calls to their helping spirits. The journeyer can ask specific helping spirits to join in the process, ask them all to join, or request the help of spirits who wish to volunteer. Sometimes the journeyer will ask a particular power animal to protect them against attaching spirits, especially if the person is entering the Middle World. We've already discussed power animals associated with the Lower World in Chapter 10.

Journeying to the Lower World

Shamans or shamanic practitioners entering the Lower World usually go down into a virtual lower Earth through a cave, tree root, waterfall, cleft in a rock—whatever takes them downward. This is an imaginal process using visualization and not a physical one of actually jumping off a waterfall or bridge!! Once in the Lower World, the journeyer typically moves downward through tunnels into large openings. They encounter subterranean rivers or lakes, animals, insects, reptiles, etc. The encounters are rarely, if ever, upsetting or fearful. The spirits of the Lower World are helpful.

Journeying to the Middle World

The Middle World, which we have talked about in Part One, is a very different place compared to the "friendlier" Lower or Upper worlds. Shamans or shamanic practitioners enter the Middle World for different reasons, such as for healing a person's spirit, emotions, psyche, or physical body; to act as a psychopomp; to inquire about the positive or negative nature of a spirit; or to heal the environment.

Whereas journeying to the Lower or Upper Worlds involves movement down or up, entry to the Middle World is simple— you are already in it! So it can be as easy as closing your eyes and visualizing yourself in Middle World space, engaging in whatever purpose you set for entering the Middle World.

The difference between journeying to the Lower or Upper Worlds and the Middle World pertains to a person's role as light-bearer. Middle World spirits can become attracted to a journey-er's light. So Shamans make sure they protect themselves before entering the Middle World and cleanse themselves after they leave.

Merging for Self-Protection from Middle World Spirits

One of the ways Shamans protect themselves to keep Middle World spirits from attaching to them while journeying is to engage in a process called "merging." Merging means that a jour-neyer asks a power animal's permission to join with it, to move their spirit into their power animal's body. It may seem novel at first. The power animal still retains its spirit but the journeyer "hitch-hikes" along with the power animal's spirit inside their body. That way, Middle World spirits don't see the journeyer or the journeyer's light; they only see the presence of a power animal. This is a tremendously effective self-protective measure!

Journeying to the Upper World

Those who journey to the Upper World go up via a tree, a tower, from a mountain top, a lofting bird, or whatever means carries them upward in their visualization. The Upper World is different because the journeyer must move through a layer of what seems like cotton candy, or a thick, dense cloud layer, something akin to a thick cobweb. The layer is there to protect the Upper World from the world of humankind in the Middle World.

In the Upper World, the journeyer may meet their spiritual mentor or a relative in order to seek guidance, an answer to a question, or healing. Some say they have met Jesus or Buddha, angels, saints, or various spirit-beings in the Upper World.

We have encountered beings who we call "light beings" or "luminaries." These beings help the spirits of departed persons find their way to the afterlife. One time they came, at our invitation, to take the spirit of our departed dog and show her where she could rest, run, and play. We are big fans of the luminaries!

Journeying to Receive Answers to Various Questions

We routinely find ourselves journeying to ask our spirit helpers a myriad of questions about such things as: the physical or mental status of a person; the source of a person's mental or physical illness; how a healing should proceed; a particular way to set up a ceremony to heal someone; whether an intrusive or negative spirit is operating; or whether we should retrieve a part of a person's psyche which may have split off due to trauma.

We've asked our helping spirits about how to handle upcoming events; for wisdom dealing with difficult people; about the nature of weather changes or patterns; even help in writing this book! The point is that journeying is a way of crossing into non-ordinary, sacred time in order to access deep knowledge of the Creator and the spirit realm.

"Biblical" Journeying/Trance States

At this point, you may be thinking that journeying to cross into non-ordinary, sacred time is not biblically approved. Well, the reality is that journeying/trances were nothing new to the Biblical world. Daniel frequently had visions during a trance-like state (Dan. 8. 18). In Acts 10, Peter fell into a trance during his noon prayer time. Paul experienced trances; he was in a trance while praying in the temple (Acts 22. 17). Later, in 2 Cor. 12. 2-4, Paul told how he was caught up into "paradise and heard inexpressible words which it is not lawful for a man to utter." And it is commonly accepted that when the Apostle John saw his visions recorded in the book of Revelation, he was in a trance state which he described as being "in the Spirit" (Rev. 4. 2; 17. 3; and 21. 10). Is it any wonder, therefore, that Jesus probably experienced a trance state when He went up the mountain to pray? If all these "biblical power hitters" experienced trance-states, we simply ask, "Why should it be a problem for us?"

It is not uncommon for people who regularly transact with Spirit to briefly shift from an ordinary to a non-ordinary reality, using their spiritual senses to check out what is going on in the spirit realm around them. This takes practice, but it becomes less and less difficult as one goes on. The goal, however, is not to induce a trance-state just for the quixotic experience. The S/spirit(s) whom we encounter in an altered state of consciousness know our hearts/motives. If they know we are serious about why we are coming into their territory, they will help us develop and deepen our altered-state experiences. They want us to be successful in serving the purposes of the Creator and helping others! But if we play around with spiritual things, those same spirits will avoid us. In addition, we may inadvertently welcome some unhealthy ones.

POWER SOUL RETRIEVAL

One of the shamanic functions is to conduct soul retrievals. What is a soul retrieval? For some people who face an extremely stressful situation, it is a common experience for their psyche to hive off part of itself for purposes of self-protection. This may seem a bit strange, but psychologically this is nothing more than a "fugue" state where the psyche compartmentalizes itself in order to protect itself from a perceived threat.

This has happened to a number of our clients, one in particular when he was younger. Situations in his childhood were drastic enough that his psyche, without his knowledge, pulled back into a defensive state and insulated a part of his nine-year-old self for the sake of self-protection. Though our client matured biologically, that part of his psyche remained suspended in a nine-year-old state until we performed a soul retrieval to bring it to the present and join it with his adult self. He now reports feeling more integrated.

Some might think it is uncommon for people to have experienced a splitting off of their psyche. But actually, it is more common than you might expect. You can hear people's awareness of this when they say, "I just don't feel like myself." "I sometimes feel like I have two people living inside me." They may say, "I feel like I'm observing the world from a distance." Or, "I feel like there's a part of me that's not good, but I can't seem to connect with it." In all these cases there is a sense of separateness within one's own person, a person within a person, that is present but detached.

To remedy a person's disconnected self, a Shaman or shamanic practitioner will journey, call to the separated soul-part, and with the self-part's permission, bring it back to be joined with the adult grown self. People who have participated in a soul retrieval often report a significant and positive shift in their sense of self, and an increased sense of happiness about their life. A felt sense of integration may not happen immediately, but it does happen eventually.

POWER RESTORATION AND EMPOWERMENT—
ACQUIRING POWER ANIMAL
PROTECTION/HELPING SPIRITS

While the spirit realm surrounds us, some people may come into direct contact with it through a negative spirit-experience. For instance, let's say a colleague cursed you in their anger. And that curse brought with it either negative energy or an actual spirit that attached to you. Or, what if you unintentionally drew in a spirit attachment by watching horror movies on a continuous basis?

Perhaps you were in a particular geographical location where spirits have attached themselves to you and you experienced unexplained harassment. Or let's say you managed to pick up some negative, non-sentient (nonliving) energy from your spouse or a friend. These are all reasons why it is helpful to have protection from the spirit realm in the form of a helping spirit/power animal. Plus, that same power animal is available to offer its wisdom and guidance anytime you need it.

We mentioned in the "Tools" chapter that some people have managed to acquire a companion or protective animal that relates to them spiritually. The majority of people, however, do not have such an animal and thus are unprotected. Nor do they know how to acquire a protective power animal that is energetically available to help them, watch over them, or give them wisdom.

The simplest way for a person to acquire a power animal would be for a Shaman or practitioner to journey for them, meet the person's power entity, return to the ordinary world with that entity, and breathe that animal essence into their client. Or, someone might opt to be trained by a Shaman to encounter a power animal for themselves! Shamans not only help people connect with a power animal (or multiple power animals) from the Lower World, they introduce their clients to helping spirits in the Upper World as well. Consider taking a workshop where you can be trained to do this activity for yourself. See our contact information at the end of the book.

EXTRACTION OF NON-SENTIENT NEGATIVE ENERGY

Because many of us think only in terms of the way we relate physically to our world, we often are not aware of energy we encounter that gets directed toward us, or that attaches to us, such as a negative morphogenic (group think) field. For example, say a person is walking through a large mall, passing numbers of people. Suddenly they feel angry or terribly depressed for no reason. They probably assume that they themselves are the source of those feelings. But upon evaluation, they might realize that they momentarily passed through someone's negative energy field and that it was the other person's feeling-state they experienced, not their own. This is an example of a non-sentient (non-spirit, nonconscious) energy field that may be present in the environment, negatively affecting us.

One of the most powerful intrusions of negative energy occurs when a person is sexually traumatized. The perpetrator often puts negative energy into or onto their victim.

A Shaman (or anyone who has worked energetically) can sense unwanted, intrusive, or negative energy in a client. The Shaman can "see" it (that is, visualize it with their mind's eye) or feel it with their hands. When we do an extraction, we note where energy shifts or where blocks are located in our client's body. We then ask our helping spirits to inform us in greater detail about these shifts or blocks. Sometimes we "see" things at those places that resemble insects or sharp objects (in an energetic, nonphysical form). On one occasion we pulled a long rod out of the head of one of our clients. The objects can be any size or shape.

Once we extract the object with our hands, we place it in an energetic container for safekeeping until we are able to dispose of the negative energy. Then we bless the person and fill them with the Spirit, goodness, light, love, etc. Most people report feeling the object removed and how different and good it feels to be clear of that negative energy.

DE-POSSESSION—EXTRACTING UNWANTED SPIRITS

We are immersed in a spirit world, a world which most of us are unable to see with our physical eyes. It is common for us to pass by spirits as we go about our day without realizing it. They generally move about doing their business. There are some spirits that are looking to attach themselves to persons for various reasons (although not too often) and they usually leave if they are asked politely. And then there are some spirits, unfortunately, who believe they have been given permission to take up residency in a person's life. These spirits can be extremely negative, even hostile. What would give them the idea they had permission to stay when invited to leave?

People who have chronic issues with addiction have been known to pick up hostile, even demonic spirits. This applies not only to substance addiction but also to sexual, food, financial, and narcissistic addictions. People who are involved in the dark arts of the occult can attract negative spirits. Let's just say that anything a person does that controls them on a long-term basis or involves them in the abuse or exploitation of others can result in a spirit/demonic infestation. The worst violent spirit we dealt with came from a person who had been assaulted, as well as getting involved with drugs and sexual behavior. A spirit transferred from one person to our client brought about a severe illness.

In de-possession, we extract the sentient (conscious) spirit. There is a certain method we use for this which has been very effective. But it is not the technique alone that makes de-possession effective. It is clear and focused intention and authority. A person doing de-possession work has to know they have authority to command a spirit to leave, once the client agrees that it must go. We tell all our clients that as followers of Christ, we operate under the authority and power of the Christ-Spirit and the Holy, Life-Giver Spirit. It is authority coupled with strong intention that makes our de-possessions work.

PSYCHOPOMP

"Psychopomp" literally means "guide of the soul." The Shaman, with the Middle World spirit's permission, aids in ushering the spirit to the Upper World. This entails approaching the deceased person's spirit, gaining its trust, finding out why it persists in the Middle World, and trying to find a way that is comfortable for the spirit to pass over to where it belongs. We have found that this kind of work may require a number of journeys, each journey moving the process along.

As we said above in our discussion of the Middle World, there are a variety of reasons some spirits remain in the Middle World. Whether they do so by choice, confusion, or fear, they find themselves "stuck" in a zone that is not ideal for them. By all accounts, they should pass on to the afterlife in the Upper World.

There are three things we have found that have made our psychopomp work successful. First, we give the Middle World spirit the opportunity to do a "trial" run where they can visit the Upper World but return to the Middle World if not happy with what they encounter. Second, we ask the Luminaries (remember them?) to meet us and the Middle World spirit when they cross over. Luminaries are full of love and acceptance; they are a great representation of beings who oversee the afterlife, Upper World experience. And third, we agree to accompany the Middle World spirit and wait for their decision to either remain in the Upper World or to return. So far, once they have encountered the Upper World, no spirit with whom we have worked has wanted to return to the Middle World.

DIVINATION

We took time in the chapter on Divination (Seven) to talk about shamanic divination. If you remember, we used Quantum Physics to present the idea that Shamans journey into the timeless, non-ordinary dimension. This allows them to see past, present, and future as a wave-potential of all possibilities. They observe a particular possibility, then set their intention to bring that possibility into the present as the highest probability.

Shamans have been doing this for millennia. It is interesting that science is now beginning to understand what Shamans have been doing intuitively. We surmise this is what Jesus was doing when He healed remotely.

Another way to view divination is through the lens of the "Aramaic Jesus" whom Neil Douglas-Klotz describes in his book, *The Hidden Gospel*.[1] In Mk. 7. 32-37, Jesus healed a deaf and dumb man. According to Douglas-Klotz, before Jesus spoke the word "*Ethphatah*" (Be Open!) in Aramaic, He looked up to heaven and breathed deeply. Douglas-Klotz tells us that Jesus' Aramaic word coupled with His glance upward and long, powerful breath revealed Jesus' connection of sound, word, thought, and action as part of one sacred unity (p. 33). And elsewhere Douglas-Klotz states that from the perspective of divine or Sacred Unity (the meaning of the word, *Alah*, or the one we refer to as God), breath is connected to all the air we breathe, which connects to the "ineffable breath [the breath of *Alah*] that pervades the seen and unseen worlds" (p. 43).

Jesus' deep and powerful breath with His upward glance, therefore, was to bring the deaf and dumb man into alignment with the Sacred Unity. In similar ways, all healers can bring others into sacred alignment with God through divination. Divination, according to this view, brings the sacred, non-ordinary "possibility" of healing into our ordinary, clock-time reality so that the two realities can be unified as a manifestation of Sacred Unity, or the One whom we refer to as Creator.

THE MESA

There are sacred circles which allow us to be brought closer to our Creator. The Mesa is like a miniature circle. Some people refer to it as their "altar." The Mesa doesn't have to be round like a stone circle. It can be a built on a small table. Personal and sacred items are placed on the Mesa, items that represent our connection to our Creator and our helping spirits, and even to our personal relationships.

On her altar and the wall above it, Sally has written words and thoughts of inspiration, crucifixes collected from her travels, a picture of the Blessed Virgin (because she has had powerful experiences with the Blessed Virgin while in Medjugorje, the shrine located in Bosnia and Herzegovina), a candle, as well as a picture of her daughter. There are various stones and objects that are energetically powerful to her, as well as some small animal fetishes which remind her of her gratitude to her helping spirits. She also has a portable mesa with other objects of significance.

Steve has two Mesas, one for travel and one on a table in his office, dedicated to his items. He will change out some of the items in the travelling Mesa depending on his intuited desire for the trip. The central object on Steve's table Mesa is a cross which came from a church in Chimayó, NM where many miracles have occurred. Other objects are simple animal fetishes symbolic of his appreciation for his relationship with his helping spirits and some beautiful stones he uses for healing.

Mesas are very personal and carry with them a great deal of power. Some Shamans place their tightly wrapped Mesa on the body of the person they are seeking to heal, or at least keep it nearby. Mesas can be made with a cloth or an animal skin used to wrap around the items it contains. We do not travel without carrying our Mesas with us, for protection and as a constant reminder of our life in the S/spirit.

ONE STEP AT A TIME

Do these advanced practices frighten you or stimulate you to learn more? We hope the latter. Our experience has been to take one step at a time in our training, integrate what we've learned with what we already know, and make sure we don't move on in our shamanic education until we have put into practice the skills and principles we have been taught. This creates a good balance of knowledge and experience, which has worked well for us.

BUDDYING UP

One more point we think is valuable to make: It is extremely helpful for a shamanic trainee to have a buddy who walks through trainings with them. A buddy offers not only encouragement but their perspective and interpretation regarding what has been taught. Our suggestion for anyone interested in acquiring shamanic training is for them to send out the intention and prayer for a companion who will move along with them through their training career.

PART III

PUTTING THE PIECES TOGETHER:
STORIES OF SUCCESS

W ell folks, we are on the home stretch of enriching your life by introducing you to shamanic practices. Our book is designed to be perused again and again. Reread sections that may confuse you or are hard to accept, and know we are always here to answer your questions. Before we part, we would like to share a short piece on healing and two inspirational stories on the healing of two of our clients. What is interesting about our two stories is that they demonstrate in full color how we do our shamanic work. But first, a word about shamanic healing.

SHAMANIC HEALING

Throughout this book we've constantly mentioned the topic of healing. As you've seen by now, healing is one of the main themes in this book and goes to the heart of how we, as authors, view the purpose of this book and our shamanic work. That is, we see ourselves as healers who want to train others how to increase their healing capacities!

Healing is a broad category that pertains to the improvement of the well-being of people—physically, cognitively, emotionally, socially, and spiritually. Since the essence of shamanic work has to do with healing, it is an easy case to make that everything that Shamans do ultimately relates to healing. And as shamanic practitioners, we endeavor to do the same: make people's lives better.

But then again, Jesus mandated His followers to do the same, to heal. And so, loving our neighbors as ourselves (another command of Jesus) dictates that compassionate healing should be at the center of our motives and actions.

Therefore, all who are committed to the well-being of others benefit by applying their life energies to healing. And specifically, it is important to learn and commit to the use of shamanic tools and practices, plus spiritual power gifts, for the purpose of healing people, society, and the environment.

In the next stories, we'd like to relay our experience in the healing of two people. We believe these stories are a good illustration of how we try to combine the use of the shamanic practices we've learned with our spiritual power gifts and our beliefs as Christ-Spirit followers. We'd like these stories to bring many of the pieces of the book together so you can see firsthand how a healing lifestyle could potentially work for you. Enjoy!

OUR SHAMANIC WORK TO HEAL BOB

Our friend Bob[1] was supposed to travel to another country but came down with a severe, migraine-like headache. It was frustrating to see his plans disrupted. Turns out, these kinds of headaches had come and gone at critically important times in our friend's life, which seemed odd.

As we do with everyone with whom we work, we queried Bob about his history. Gathering history gives us a multidimensional way of understanding how certain conditions develop in or around people. We learned he had been involved in an auto accident where an elderly man had come out of nowhere to plow into him. Again, an odd occurrence to us. The auto accident had exacerbated our friend's headaches. This made us wonder if the auto accident was instigated by a negative spirit.

Questioning him as to when the headaches initially began to occur, Bob shared that in his mid-twenties he had been living with his twin brother, their mother, and their paternal grandmother. Bob thought that his grandmother was being too controlling toward his mother and told her to back off. Early the next morning, without notice or provocation, Bob's twin entered his bedroom and punched him hard on his face/jaw. This caused Bob's neck to snap back and injure his C2-C3 vertebrae. And the rest, shall we say, was history.

Remember Paul Harvey's radio broadcast which ended, "And now, the rest of the story"? Well, there's more "story" with our friend because sometimes things that seem too odd tend to point a finger toward some kind of spirit-activity.

Bob shared that his brother's actions weren't too out of the ordinary because it was common for his family members to act violently toward each other. Apparently, this kind of behavior went far back in his family's history. With any of our clients, when we learn that violence or medical conditions have come down through previous generations, it is a strong indication that we are dealing with a familial spirit and, in Bob's case, one that was potentially violent.

So, this is where our shamanic process began. The great thing about shamanic work is that we didn't need to "guess" if we were dealing with a generational spirit. We could journey (with Bob's permission) and find out.

We have already explained the practice of journeying between the worlds. In this instance, we went into the Middle World and called to Bob's spirit. Before we journeyed, we asked our helping spirits to accompany us, and to offer us their helpful perceptions and protection. On our journey, we saw (visualized) a dark mass, a negative entity, connected to the side of Bob's neck, around the C2-C3 area. Further journeywork showed us that this spirit had entered the family line many generations before.

We knew we would need to extract it. For us, "extraction" is the removal of non-sentient energy. If the energy is sentient, it must agree to go voluntarily. "De-possession" is the vacating of a sentient spirit that will not leave voluntarily. How was this spirit going to leave, voluntarily or involuntarily? We did more journeying and talked directly to the spirit.

Shamans have different views on conversing with a spirit. Some Shamans recommend never conversing with a spirit, just removing it. We have a different method. We've learned that it is helpful to learn from the spirits themselves why they arrived, what gave them permission to stay, what their purpose was for attaching to our client and, when they leave, where they want to go. We remind the spirit that it cannot lie to us because we command it, through the authority of Christ-Jesus, to tell the truth and that it must answer all our questions. No fudging allowed!

The other important thing we do when working with the extraction of a sentient spirit is to fast for at least a day before an extraction. Fasting tunes us up spiritually and gives us a super-focused ability to discern what is taking place. So in Bob's case, we had a chat with this spirit, gained knowledge, and fasted.

On the day of our ceremony and extraction, we were ready to rock and roll. We opened sacred space, invited in our Godhead and helping spirits, and began our method of doing the actual extraction. This method involves using two large crystals. However, when we tried to speak to the spirit and move it into the crystals, Steve couldn't locate it. It had gone to sleep or decided to "play possum."

Sally used her intuition and perception to locate the spirit, which had lodged in another part of Bob's body (it had moved away from the neck). Steve asked one of his helping spirits who is associated with fire to "turn up the heat" on the spirit in order to motivate it to leave. Shortly afterward, the spirit, who didn't like the fire lit under it, moved out and into the crystals. Mission accomplished.

We share this story because it involved several shamanic activities:

- First, perception—sensing that something was odd with our friend's condition and that there were too many strange instances to be accounted for by the physical world alone.
- Second, journeying to determine if there was a spirit and what kind of spirit was working.
- Third, learning what gave the spirit an opportunity to attach itself.
- Fourth, an extraction, which could be done ceremonially in different ways, once we determined which way was appropriate.
- Fifth, working with the negative spirit to place it, hopefully, in a higher level of vibration where it could begin to do good.
- Sixth, working with power gifts—the Word of Knowledge and the Word of Wisdom—which we defined in the chapter on Spiritual Power Gifts.

The happy ending to the story is this. Since the extraction, Bob has never experienced any more severe migraine headaches! This is the power of combining shamanic tools with spiritual power gifts.

OUR SHAMANIC WORK TO HEAL TINA

In our work, we combine a number of practices: life-coaching; cognitive-emotive therapy; bio-energy/massage therapy; shamanic tools/practices (journeying, extraction, empowerment, de-possession, chakra balancing); spiritual (power) gifts of wisdom, knowledge, discernment, and healing; worship and prayer. You will see these tools used at various times and in various ways as we share about Tina.[2] Sometimes our work is completed in one session. Other times, transformation occurs over multiple sessions as layers of healing occur over time, as with Tina.

Tina came to us at the recommendation of a friend who was acquainted with our work. Tina was depressed, largely due to a feeling of insecurity she developed because she had been abandoned by her mother at an early age. We began by using some life coaching skills of listening, gathering information, and validating her as a person.

After several beginning sessions, we explained to Tina that we worked using the help of the Spirit and that as followers of the Christ-Spirit, we would be calling on Spirit to help heal her depression. Because Tina welcomed working with Spirit, we began our sessions by opening sacred space with different shamanic tools, inviting the Christ-Spirit and the Life-Giver Spirit to come.

We spent time talking with Tina from a cognitive perspective about her false beliefs in herself, how she had come to develop them, and how she might begin to think differently about herself. We gave Tina a paper that provided Scripture verses of the positive ways God sees her and asked that she begin to view herself from that perspective. As her treatment progressed, we encouraged Tina to consider adding a meditation practice to her prayer life: to establish a place of calmness, give herself a time to practice reflecting on the positive changes she was making, and interact with and acquire wisdom from her helping spirits. Tina continues this practice now on a consistent basis.

There was a particular traumatizing incident that caused Tina to split off part of herself at about the age of eight. We used a therapeutic technique to minimize the traumatic event. Then eventually, and after careful explanation, we conducted a Soul Retrieval so that we could work with a complete self, not a bifurcated one.

Tina had been involved in some male relationships which were not beneficial to her or her children. We began, as life coaches, to show Tina how these prior relationships fit perfectly like jig-saw pieces with her poor view of herself. Tina began to realize that she was not a bad person, she had merely made poor relationship decisions as a result of some incidents in her childhood. As part of our opening sacred space, we drummed and asked Tina to visualize herself, healed and empowered. She also kept a journal, writing down the things she learned during our sessions.

At this point we introduced Tina to the concept of empowerment, utilizing helping spirits in the form of power animals. In her meditation time, Tina had already associated with both a Jaguar and a Panda Bear. We urged her to call on those helping spirits whenever she felt down or in doubt. Tina grew to rely more and more on the confidence those helping spirits gave her.

There were times Tina reported feeling like she had retreated into her old, negative way of thinking and feeling about herself. We handled this by smudging Tina and sharing words of knowledge about the positive qualities we saw in her. Sometimes we used our hands to project the smoke and intention, and other times we used feathers. One time we used our Tibetan singing bowl to calm Tina's energy. Many times we drummed for Tina, using positive words of knowledge about her character to fill her aura and encourage her spirit.

At a turning point, we thought it would be helpful to balance Tina's chakras.[3] The word "chakra" is a Hindu term which means "whirling." There are seven major meridian points associated with the midline of the body where energy enters and feeds vitality to our organs, mind, and spirit. Some of Tina's chakras were not spinning in the right direction and we remedied this.

Another time we extracted negative energy from Tina. It is a common misconception that memory is only stored in our brain. Actually, it is stored not only in the brain but in various parts of the body. Tina's body had several locations where she had acquired and stored negative energy. We not only extracted those negative energies but did some bio-energetic work to balance her body's energy (different from chakra balancing). Tina reported feeling relieved.

Our involvement with Tina has continued over many months. When we started, our work was curative, but now it is becoming more and more supportive. Also, as we have moved along, Tina is adopting some of the shamanic tools we introduced her to and is using them to empower herself.

Tina's story shows that a gentle fusion of methods combined to heal Tina's whole person:[4]

- First, observation and perception. Gathering background information provides a wholistic view of a person's past and present. It provides an awareness of the spiritual forces working in Tina's life that benefit or hold her back.
- Second, life-coaching. While listening to Tina's struggles, we always held out hope for positive change and self-empowerment, directing Tina's perspective toward a beneficial future.
- Third, opening sacred space, smudging, drumming, playing a Tibetan bowl, and helping spirit (power animal) empowerment enabled Tina to become increasingly involved with the S/spirit world as part of her healing.
- Fourth, extraction of negative energies, chakra balancing, and bio-energetic body balancing.
- Fifth, spiritual discussion that encouraged the use of Tina's faith-perspective for the sake of her self-empowerment. This involved coaching Tina on techniques such as meditation, prayer, visualization, smudging, singing, etc.
- Sixth, power soul retrieval. Uniting a person with their split-off self.

When we first began our work, we were unsure if it was

possible to combine our different professional training and back-grounds with our shamanic practices and spiritual gifts. But we are happy to report that all of this has come together quite powerfully, not only for us but for our clients as well. It is exciting to have so many tools at our disposal and to be able to pick the perfect one, rather than having only one set of tools and hoping they can fit the client's needs.

In other words, combine the use of shamanic tools with your life training and experiences. Add them to your faith-practices of prayer, healing, worship, and spiritual gifts. By doing so, you will be able to extend a powerful blessing to others from the Creator, Christ-Spirit, and spirit realm. Not only can you facilitate healing in another person, but that positive energy also will ripple out to support healing and goodness in the world! What an exciting difference you can make by learning and utilizing these gifts!

13

WRAPPING UP

Take a minute and think about where you started when you began reading this book. Were you pro-Shamanism? Did you think that truth could only be "Christian" to be valid when there is truth to be found everywhere in the universe if we look for it?

Did you have doubts about whether you could allow yourself to entertain the possibility of associating your beliefs with shamanic practices, no matter what your faith perspective is? Are you surprised you have a growing interest in learning more about Shamanism?

We've been holding loving space through our prayers for anyone who reads our book. We know what it is like for people when "deep" calls them "to deep," when the truths we've presented reach inside and call them to new levels of growth and higher states of spiritual understanding. But it isn't us who has been calling—it is S/spirit.

Perhaps you are new to this lifestyle but excited to move on to this path. Good. Welcome, we believe there's no better place to be. Sometimes, however, it may feel like you are swimming against the flow of your cultural current, friends, or even your church. Well, keep swimming! It is worth it.

There are some Christians who will read this document, walk away and say: "I don't care what you write, helping spirits are demonic. I want nothing to do with them!!" For those who do, we point you to 1 Corinthians 10 with a word of exhortation.

The Apostle Paul addressed the issue of marketplace meat that possibly had been offered to idols (demons, 1 Cor. 10. 25). But he told the Corinthian Christians: 'Go ahead and eat the meat because the meat is from an animal created by God, and God is greater than any idol: "the earth is the Lord's and all its fullness"' (v. 26). Paul said, bless the food (meat), give thanks, and partake all to the glory of God (v. 30-31).

There was for Paul, however, a caveat. It had to do with conscience. If someone who was not a Christian informed the Christian person that the meat had been offered to idols, Paul said, "Do not eat it for the sake of the one who told you, for conscience' sake" (v. 28). Otherwise, "partake" with thanksgiving and don't judge or speak evil of others who do (v. 30).

In the same way, (helping) spirits are the Lord's and the fullness of the universe belongs to Him. There is no reason we can't invite helping spirits to come to our aid, and with their help to heal people and then give glory to God!

Some Christians feel comfortable interacting responsibly with spirits (possibly through Shamanism), and some don't. For those Christians who don't feel comfortable, they should not "partake" for the sake of their conscience. But for those Christians who do feel comfortable "partaking" with positive, helping spirits, let us not judge or speak evil of them for the reasons Paul cited in 1 Corinthians 10.

And remember, "The Earth is the Lord's and all its fullness" (Ps. 24. 1). There is no need to fear spirits because God is the Creator of all beings. Once you experience the power of intuitive listening and get your spiritual senses turned on, you will receive the confirmation you need when you cross into the sacred, non-ordinary spirit realm. Remember our quote from Fred Alan Wolf: we see when we believe. As a result, you will experience wisdom and power like you have never had before. You will never do things the same way.

LET'S RECAP

You have come a long way, learning that we all tune into the same Spirit, the Christ-Spirit. The very elements of the creation are sentient and have a voice not only to worship their Creator-Christ but to speak to us as well.

Now you know that you can access the spirit realm to connect to positive, helping spirits who want to help you heal and help people. These helping spirits are spirit-beings who are before the throne of God but are part of our world as well.

Who would have ever considered that Jesus performed many "shamanic" functions during His life, or concluded that He is the Ultimate Shaman? Jesus is a model for us, one who lived His life being directed by Spirit and moving in its power.

And by now, we hope you are considering how to turn on your spiritual intuition and listening capacities. Maybe you are thinking hard about escaping the trap of rationalism and allowing your heart to connect with the non-ordinary/sacred-spirit realm through journeying or meditation.

S/spirit-filled life is to be lived actively with full use of your spiritual gifts. In other words, you may have picked up a few shamanic tools and, coupled with some power gifts, you can use them to free friends and family who are held in bondage to spirits, negative energies, physical maladies, or destructive lifestyles. How wonderful is that?

Perhaps you've come to the conclusion that it's time to press on, to become more interactive with the spirit realm, putting aside fear or reservation. You are considering getting into a training program that can school you in the use of various advanced shamanic practices. From our perspective, why wouldn't you? See below for our outreach information. We would love to connect with you.

Thanks for taking this journey with us. We'd like to think this book has opened a door for you to the spirit world. If you are interested, step through it! Don't be shy. Listening to S/spirit and actively practicing a life of spirit-awareness, power, and action trains you to live a life that is powerful and will result not only in healing and freedom for yourself, but for many others—if you commit yourself to that lifestyle. Let's develop and expand our God-given spiritual senses and participate in the larger life that God, the Christ-Spirit, intended for every one of us.

CONTACT INFORMATION FOR TRANSFORMING LIVES

We have established an outreach called *Transforming Lives*. Here's how you can reach us if you are interested in continuing our conversation about bridging the gap and entering a deeper healing with Spirit. We hope you do!

- Send us an email at: transforminglives29@gmail.com. We will add you to our database, or let you know when some of our trainings are scheduled.
- Find us on Facebook at: **@transformin- glivesBullDenny**. From time to time we publish short pieces that help people to advance their spirit-living.
- Check out our website: http://www.**transforming- lives.us**. Our webpage is a great place to contact us with questions, to learn more about bridging to Shamanism through our workshops. There you will find our treatment/healing goals and perspectives. We share short, informative pieces we've created in our blog.
- Contract with us for our healing services.

ABOUT THE AUTHORS

STEVE BULL

Steve holds a Masters of Divinity and a Masters of (Clinical) Social Work. He worked as a Christian missionary for 16 years, pioneering two works: in the inner city of San Francisco as an outreach to impoverished Central American refugees; the other in the remote parts of Eastern Oregon to cowboys and ranchers. Following his ministries, Steve worked as a psychotherapist for 19 years, holding a license in Clinical Social Work. Steve also functioned as a Social Worker and Chaplain for Hospice over a number of years.

Experiences in ministry, psychotherapy, and hospice motivated Steve to integrate his understanding of spirituality, religion, and his professional training through the study of Shamanism. How are people healed who are deeply, traumatically wounded on a soul/spirit basis, such as the veterans with whom Steve worked? How do people grow and enhance a connection with their spirit during their lifetime and then easily cross to the next life? How are people physically healed by working with their spirit in the physical/spirit realms? These and other questions have excited Steve's heart and mind and continually led him to learn and access the spirit world. The authorship of this book has come out of the deep questioning that provoked Steve's thinking.

SALLY DENNY

Sally has had an intimate connection with the spirit realm since childhood. Being involved in leadership capacities within the Catholic and Protestant churches she attended through the years, Sally has led retreats, seminars, Bible studies, and liturgical gatherings in lay and staff positions. For the last twenty years she has worked as a licensed massage and bodywork therapist. Sally's private practice therapies are based on bioenergetics and polarity, which are ways of connecting and balancing the body's energies, to bring both physical and life challenges into balance. She brings the power of Spirit into each client's sessions, working to bring wholeness through intuitive and claircognizant healing. Sally enjoys time with her animals, family and friends, baking and cooking delicious foods, and creating beauty in her Sonoran Desert home environment.

BIBLIOGRAPHY

Brown, F.; Driver, S.; and Briggs, C. *A Hebrew and English Lexicon of the Old Testament*. Hendrickson, Rev. 1996.

Bull, Stephen. *Supernatural Powers in the Heavenly Realms*. Printed by the Author, 1998.

Clinton, James R. *Spiritual Gifts*. Horizon House Publishers, 1985.

DeWaay, Bob. *The Dangers of Divination*. http://www.deceptioninthechurch.com/dangersofdivination.html.

Divination: Definition of Divination. Merriam-Webster. https://www.merriam:webster.com/dictionary/divination

Douglas-Klotz, N. *The Hidden Gospel: Decoding the Spiritual Message of the Aramaic Jesus*. Quest, 1999.

Ford, Paul R. *Unleash Your Church: Mobilizing Spiritual Gifts Series*. Charles E. Fuller Institute, 1993.

Fuller, Robert C. *Spiritual, But Not Religious: Understanding Unchurched America*. Oxford University Press, 2001.

Harner, Michael. *The Way of the Shaman*; Tenth Anniversary Edition. Harper, San Francisco, 1990.

Hayford, Jack W., Gen. Editor. *Spirit Filled Life Bible*, New King James Version. Thomas Nelson, 1991.

Heiser, Michael S. *Angels*. Lexham Press, 2018.

Heiser, Michael S. *The Unseen Realm: Recovering the Supernatural Worldview of the Bible*. Lexham Press, 2015.

Linderman, Frank B. *Plenty Coups: Chief of the Crows*. University of Nebraska Press, 2002.

Necromancy: https://en.wikipedia.org/wiki/Necromancy.

Neihardt, John G. *Black Elk Speaks: The Complete Edition*. University of Nebraska Press, 2014.

Padfield, David. *The Abominations of the Canaanites*. https://padfield.com/acrobat/history/canaanite-abominations.pdf, 2009.

Science Daily. *Brain Waves and Meditation*. The Norwegian University of Science and Technology, 2010. https://www.sciencedaily.com/releases/2010/03/100319210631.htm.

Sheldrake, R. *Morphic Resonance and Morphic Fields—an Introduction*. https://sheldrake.org/research/morphic-resonance/introduction.

Stevens, José. L. *Awaken the Inner Shaman: A Guide to the Power Path of the Heart*. Sounds True, 2014.

Stevens, José Luis and Stevens, Lena. *The Power Path Training;
Living the Secrets of the Inner Shaman*; Sounds True, 2014. Session 1,
Tracks 2 & 3.

The Foundation for Shamanic Studies. https://
wwwshamanism.org/index.php.

Theta Healing; Theta Brain State. https://www.thetahealing.com/
about-thetahealing/thetahealing-theta-state.html.

Virkler, Mark and Patti. *"Communion with God: Student's Study
Manual."* Destiny Image Publishers, PO Box 351, Shippensburg,
PA, 17257, 1983.

Wolf, Fred Alan. *The Eagle's Quest: A Physicist's Search for Truth in
the Heart of the Shamanic World.* Summit Books, 1991.

NOTES

ACKNOWLEDGMENTS

1. In this book we refer to the Spirit in a number of ways: Holy Spirit, the Holy Spirit, Spirit, the Spirit, the Great Spirit, and Life-Giver Spirit (the Spirit who gives life to all sentient beings). The Spirit, Holy Spirit, or Great Spirit is referred to in different ways by various cultures. We try to be inclusive and respectful of the ways Spirit is referred to in diverse cultures.

ABBREVIATIONS

1. Hayford, Jack W., Gen. Editor. *Spirit Filled Life Bible*, New King James Version. Thomas Nelson, 1991.

1. SHAMANISM AND CHRISTIAN PRACTICE

1. Stevens, José Luis and Stevens, Lena. *The Power Path Training: Living the Secrets of the Inner Shaman*; Sounds True, 2014. Session 1, Tracks 2 & 3.
2. Broadly, "helping spirits" are ones who make their wisdom and power available to "help us" heal. They work under the authority and power of the Holy Spirit. We will go into more detail about "helping spirits" and their benefit to us in a later chapter.
3. Harner, Michael. *The Way of the Shaman*; Tenth Anniversary Edition. Harper, San Francisco, 1990; p. 20.
4. Stevens, José Luis and Stevens, Lena. *The Power Path Training*; Session 1, Tracks 2 & 3.
5. Stevens, José Luis and Stevens, Lena. *The Power Path* Training; Session 1, Tracks 2 & 3.

2. THE "SHAMANIC" PRACTICES OF JESUS

1. In commenting on the shamanic relevance of Jesus' vision quest, the goal is not to minimize the seminal importance of what occurred during those forty days of fasting and temptation regarding the preparation of Jesus for His ministry. If Jesus had given in to the temptation of Satan, it would have been "game over." No need to die on the cross, no need for the resurrection.

2. Neihardt, John G. *Black Elk Speaks: The Complete Edition.* University of Nebraska Press, 2014; pp. 13-29.
3. Neihardt, John G. *Black Elk Speaks;* pp. 153-154. "Against the tree there was a man standing with arms held wide in front of him. I looked hard at him, and I could not tell what people he came from. He was not a *Wasichu* (White man) and he was not an Indian. His hair was long and hanging loose, and on the left side of his head he wore an eagle feather. His body was strong and good to see, and it was painted red. I tried to recognize him but I could not make him out. He was a very fine looking man. While I was staring hard at him, his body began to change and become very beautiful with all colors of light and around him there was a light. He spoke like singing: 'My life is such that all earthly beings and growing things belong to me. Your father, the Great Spirit, has said this. You too must say this.'"
4. Linderman, Frank B. *Plenty Coups: Chief of the Crows.* University of Nebraska Press, 2002; pp. 34-37.
5. Mt. 15. 21-28; Mk. 7. 24-30; Jn. 4. 46-53.
6. In the future we will refer to the combination of the work of the Holy Spirit and our helping spirits as S/spirit.
7. Verses for the bullets in the main text: He had power (Mt. 11. 28-30); to fulfill prophecy that the Messiah would remove people's infirmities (Is. 53. 4-5; Mt. 8. 16-17); to show His direct relationship with His Father (Jn.10. 37-38); to release people from their infirmities caused by evil spirits and Satan (Acts 10. 38; 1 Jn. 38). Much to their dismay, Jesus healed to show the theocrats that man-made laws could not prevent Him from dispensing mercy when their man-made laws prohibited it (Lk. 6. 1-5; 14. 1-6); to demonstrate He had the power to forgive sin (Mk. 2. 8-9); and to glorify His Father (Jn. 10. 37-38).
8. Compassionate healing: Mt. 8. 3; 9. 36; 14. 14; 15. 29-39; 18. 11-13, 33; 20. 29-34; Mk. 1. 40-42; 6. 30-44; 8. 2-3; 9. 22; Lk. 7. 13-14; 15. 11-32; 19. 41-42; Jn. 8. 8-9.
9. Jesus' reliance on the Spirit: Acts 10. 38; Jn. 3. 34; 5. 19-20; 10. 37; 12. 49. The Spirit descended on Jesus at His baptism (Lk. 3. 22). Jesus was led by the Spirit into the desert to fast and be tempted (Mk. 1. 12; Lk. 4. 1). Jesus returned from His forty-day fast to begin His ministry "in the power of the Spirit" (Lk. 4. 14). The power of the Spirit was present for Jesus to heal the sick (Lk. 5. 17; 6. 19). Jesus cast out demons by the power of God (Mt. 12. 28). Jesus was full of joy through the Holy Spirit (Lk. 10. 21). God anointed Jesus with the Holy Spirit (Acts 10. 38; Heb. 1. 9).

3. TWO SOURCES OF SHAMANIC WISDOM

1. "The Lord possessed me at the beginning of His way, before His works of old. I have been established from everlasting, from the beginning before there was ever an earth" (Prov. 8. 22-23).

2. Chaldeans were known as Kasdites, originating in Kesed, a region in lower Mesopotamia. They were renowned as astrologers and astronomers and considered the wisest of people.

3. Pharisees were a social/religious movement with great political power that functioned from the Second Temple period on and were present during the life of Jesus and the early church: https://en.wikipedia.org/wiki/Pharisees.

4. 1 Kgs. 22. 19; Ps. 82. 1, 6; 89. 5-7; 97. 9; Heb. 12. 22; Rev. 5. 11; 7. 11.

5. Brown, F.; Driver, S.; and Briggs, C. *A Hebrew and English Lexicon of the Old Testament*. Hendrickson, Rev. 1996; p. 43. The *elohim* of Ps. 8. 1, 6 are categorized as rulers, judges, either as divine representatives at sacred places or as reflecting divine majesty and power.

6. Heiser, Michael S. *The Unseen Realm: Recovering the Supernatural Worldview of the Bible*. Lexham Press, 2015; p. 33.

7. See also Ps. 68. 17; Rev. 5.

8. There are between 100 billion to 400 billion stars in the Milky Way galaxy alone. There are approximately 100 billion galaxies in the universe. A conservative estimate of 100 billion stars in the Milky Way x 100 billion galaxies = 10 sextillion stars, or 1×10^{22}. If we say, hypothetically, that spirits are attached to only 1/8 of the stars in the universe (that's not counting any planets), that's still a whole lot of zeroes (1.25×10^{21}). In other words, there are an immense number of spirits in the universe. Is it too much to believe that some of these might be given the role of helpers of humanity?

9. Heiser, Michael S. *Angels*. Lexham Press, 2018; p. 57.

10. Heiser, Michael S. *Angels*; p. 57.

11. Heiser, Michael S. *Angels*; p. 28, pp. 1-56. Heiser, in his well-researched book, *Angels*, writes that the word "angel" refers to its function and not to its ontology (essence), which is spirit. Non-earthly, heavenly "spirits" function in multiple ways, such as: messengers (mal'ak/angelos), ministers, watchers, mighty ones (in Yahweh's celestial army), mediators, or cherubim and seraphim.

12. Some Pharisees challenged Jesus' disciples for saying, "Blessed is the King who comes in the name of the Lord! Peace in heaven and glory in the highest." Jesus responded, "I tell you that if these should keep silent, the stones would immediately cry out" (Lk. 19. 40). Was Jesus speaking figuratively? We think not; we believe He meant it. The stones have the spirit of their Creator in them. That is why they would cry out.

Paul tells us in Romans 8 that the present time does not compare to the glory that is to come. As a result, the creation is essentially in the pangs of labor, waiting to be "delivered from the bondage of corruption into the glorious liberty of the children of God" (Rom. 8. 19-21). In other words, the creation knows itself, has a sense about itself, and has a sense about its destiny in the purposes of God.

Admitting that the elements of the creation have spirits attached to them is not pantheism, any more than the Psalms which speak about a heavenly council of "gods." It simply means that the life breathed into the creation by the Christ-Spirit has a consciousness, an awareness. It not only worships God but it speaks to us if we are listening.

The spirits of the creation are not meant to be worshipped any more than angels are.

13. Even Jesus said that if the people blessing His coming in the name of the Lord were to stop their praises, the stones would immediately cry out (Lk. 19. 40).

14. The Second Temple/Intertestamental period was the time between the Old and New Testaments, spanning roughly 400 years, from Malachi (the last Old Testament prophet) to John the Baptist. The Israelites had returned to Judah and built the second temple (the first was destroyed by Nebuchadnezzar). During this time, the following literature appeared: Greek translations of the Old Testament (called the Septuagint, or LXX), the Dead Sea Scrolls (DSS), Rabbinic Literature, Philo, Targums, the Apocrypha and the Pseudepigrapha.

List of Apocrypha: Tobit, Judith, Addition to the Book of Esther, Wisdom of Solomon, Wisdom of Joshua ben Sira, Baruch, Letter of Jeremiah, Addition to the Book of Daniel, Prayer of Azariah, the Song of the Three Jews, Susanna, Bel and the Dragon; 1, 2, 3, 4 Maccabees; 1 &2 Esdras, Prayer of Manasseh, Ps. 151.

List of Pseudepigrapha: Apocalypse of Abraham, Books of Adam and Eve, Apocalypse of Adam, Syriac Apocalypse of Baruch, Biblical Antiquities, Book of Enoch, Book of the Secrets of Enoch, Fourth Book of Esdras, Books of Giants, Book of Jubilees, Lives of the Prophets, Testament of Moses (Assumption of), Testament of Solomon, Testaments of the Twelve Patriarchs.

15. Heiser, Michael S. *Angels*, pp. 88-89.

16. Heiser, Michael S. *The Unseen Realm*; footnote, p. 24.

17. Some people may associate the terms "guardian spirit" or "helping spirits" with "guardian angels." There is no specific reference to the phrase "guardian angel" in the Bible. Heb. 1. 14 tells us that angels are spirits sent to minister to (serve) those who will inherit salvation. According to Ps. 91.1-2, 11-12, those who abide under the shadow of the Almighty, who say, 'I will say of the Lord, "He is my refuge and my fortress; My God, in Him I will trust,"' the promise is made that "He [God] shall give His angels charge over you, to keep you in all your ways. In their hands He shall bear you up, lest you dash your foot against a stone."

Jesus seemed to indicate in Mt. 18.10 that even little children have "guardian" angels who "see the face of My Father who is in heaven." It is believed Peter's [guardian] angel helped him escape from prison (Acts 12.5-15). Ps. 34.7 says: "The angel of the Lord encamps all around those who fear Him [God] and delivers them."

Let the reader decide if the term "guardian" angel is preferrable to "helping spirit." In either case, it appears that the angel/spirit has been tasked with the positive job of protecting those who are committed to their Creator.

Even though Harner talks about acquiring a "guardian" spirit, the most common spirits to whom people in the shamanic field refer are called helping spirits or allies. For our purposes in this book, we will refer to helping spirits rather than guardian spirits or guardian angels.

Sally makes the point that the helping spirits with whom she deals in Shamanism are not the same as her experiences with angels.

"I've encountered angels on a few occasions, none of which was by my initiation. Each encounter occurred when they came to me; I wasn't looking for them. In each circumstance when they appeared, the energy in the air changed and became electrified. All the hair on my body stood on end.

"My awareness was that I was in the presence of a very powerful, divine Being. Each Being was very large in stature. For example, once in my kitchen one took the form of a male and stood as high as the ceiling. I felt fearful and at the same time humbled because it was obvious this angel meant business. Each encounter was a very intense experience and each angel had a specific message for me.

"In contrast, the helping spirits I encounter in my journeys are wise, truth-filled, ready and willing to assist me. They do not exude power as the angels do but are strong and confident in their own selves. I go to them requesting information. However, on some occasions, they do come to me with messages. They take on different appearances, sometimes as an animal, sometimes in human likeness, always in spirit essence. But there is no comparison between being in the presence of my helping spirits and a powerful angel. They are very separate types of entities."

4. ONLY THE HOLY SPIRIT, HELPING SPIRITS, OR BOTH?

1. If we used only the rules of logic to prove the existence of helping spirits, we wouldn't blame anyone for concluding that this is nothing more than a "thought experiment" and walking away. But in addition to instances recorded in the Bible of angels "helping" people, we can say that not only we, but thousands of shamanic practitioners constantly experience the help and presence of helping spirits.
2. Heiser, Michael S. *The Unseen Realm*; p. 32.
3. Heiser, Michael S. *Angels*; pp. 120-1.

5. THE WORLD AS SHAMANS AND CHRISTIANS SEE IT. WHO IS RIGHT?

1. This is a good time to state that we do not consider ourselves to be Shamans and never refer to ourselves as such. We simply say that we are shamanic practitioners.

2. While this document doesn't allow the length needed to expound on the topic of the war being waged in the heavenly realms, we will make a quick overview using material from: Bull, Stephen. *Supernatural Powers in the Heavenly Realms*. Self-Published, 1998.

The Principalities seem to rule with the Powers, exactly how we do not know. They are attached to nations, various levels of government, and institutions of power. Their presence is localized to the earth. Because they are enemies of God (1 Cor. 15. 24-25), together they influence their human counterparts to govern in ways that are counter to the purposes of God.

Look at Dan. 10. 12-13 where the angel Gabriel was prevented by the "prince of Persia" (probably a Principality) from bringing Daniel a revelation. The help of Michael, an archangel, was required to overcome the Persian angelic prince.

The world rulers are dark because they are associated with the rule of Satan, whose person and mission are described as darkness (Lk. 22. 53; Jn. 3. 19; Acts 26. 18; Rom. 13. 12; 2 Cor. 6. 14; Col. 1. 13; 1 Thess. 5. 5; 1 Pet. 2. 9) and of "this age" (Mt. 4. 16; Lk. 1. 79; Jn. 1. 5; 8. 12; 12. 35, 46; 2 Cor. 6. 14; Eph. 5. 11; 1 Thess. 5. 5), which is evil (Gal. 1. 4; Eph. 5. 16; 6. 13).

Col. 1. 16 is the only citation where "dominions" (plural) are mentioned in the New Testament. Since Principalities and Powers are often coupled, we might consider "thrones and dominions" as a couplet which refer to an even higher class of spirits that rule, like the Revelation elders, in the higher heavens.

"Air" is another word for "stronghold"—thought patterns and ideas generated/directed by evil, spiritual beings. Whether the atmosphere of Satanic thought patterns and ideas influences our personal thinking or becomes part of our social institutions, the result is the same—churches, communities, and nations governed by false "strongholds" (concepts contrary to the purposes and will of God) move people away from God.

Satan had a throne (position of authority) in heaven at one time (Is. 14. 13) from which he quite probably governed the *Elohim*-of-the-nations (Principalities and Powers). He was incredibly wise (Ezek. 28. 17) but more interested in exalting himself than fulfilling his role as God's number one cherub. He began to "divine" himself, forcing subordinate spiritual entities to prostrate themselves before him.

God brought forth fire from Satan's midst which devoured him, turning him to ashes (an appropriate punishment since he sinned because of his prideful desire to increase his beauty (Is. 12. 17; 1 Tim. 3. 6)) and cast him to earth (Ezek. 28. 18; Is. 14. 12).

When Satan was cast to earth, however, he did not lose his authority. That is why Jesus called Satan the "ruler of this world" (Jn. 12. 31; 14. 30; 16. 11), and why Paul referred to him as the "prince of the power of the air, the spirit who now works in the sons of disobedience" (Eph. 2. 2), the "god of this age" (2 Cor. 4. 4). Therefore Luke 4. 5-6 refers to Satan's authority over the angelic rulers of the kingdoms of the world (the Principalities and Powers), many of whom are evil and conspire with Satan.

If the reader desires a more thorough theological investigation and discussion regarding the concepts above, read: Heiser, Michael. *The Unseen Realm: Recovering the Supernatural Worldview of the Bible*. Heiser's work is exhaustive but eye-opening and well worth the detailed read.

3. While teaching in a synagogue in Capernaum, Jesus ordered the spirit to be quiet and come out of the man. (Mk. 1. 21-28; Lk. 4. 31-37).

Jesus sent a "legion" of demons possessing a man (Matthew reports two men) into a nearby herd of swine, which ran down a steep bank into the sea and drowned (Mt. 8. 28-34; Mk. 5. 1-20; Lk 8. 26-39).

After Jesus drove a demon out of a person who was mute, restoring their speech, He was accused of driving out demons by the power of Beelzebub (the devil) (Mt. 12. 22-32; Mk. 3. 20-30; Lk. 11. 14-26).

Many demons were coming out of people. Jesus rebuked them and ordered them not to speak because they knew He was the Messiah (Lk. 4. 41).

In Mt. 17. 14-20; Mk. 9. 14-29; Lk. 9. 37-43, Jesus' disciples were unable to cast out a demon from a man's son. Jesus ordered the spirit to leave the boy. The demon made the boy convulse, and with a cry, left.

A Greek woman went to Jesus and asked him to drive out a demon from her daughter. At first he refused but when she persisted He said, "O woman, great is your faith! Let it be done for you as you wish." When she returned home, the demon had, in fact, left her daughter (Mt. 15. 21-28; Mk 7. 24-30).

Both the Gospels of Mark and Luke describe Mary Magdalene as someone out of whom Jesus had driven seven demons (Mk. 16. 9; Lk. 8. 2).

Jesus sent out his disciples to spread the gospel of the kingdom, giving them power to drive out all demons/unclean spirits (Mk. 6. 7; Mt. 10. 1; Lk. 9. 1).

After His resurrection, Jesus gave power to all His followers to cast out demons (Mk. 16. 17).

Demons also caused people an inordinate amount of pain, sorrow, and suffering: Disease or illness (Lk. 8. 2; Mt. 10. 1; Lk. 13. 11; Acts 8. 7; 19. 12); dumbness (Mt. 9. 32; Lk. 11. 14); deafness and dumbness (Mt. 12. 22); blindness and dumbness (Mt. 12. 22); convulsions (Mk. 9. 20; Lk. 9. 42); paralysis/lameness (Acts 8. 7); the possession of children, resulting in: violent, anti-social behavior (Mt. 8. 28; Lk. 8. 27, 29; Acts 19. 16); terrible suffering (Mt. 15. 22) and torment (1 Sam. 16. 14; Acts 5. 16); epilepsy with self-destructive behavior (Mt. 17. 15); super-human, yet self-destructive strength (Mk. 5. 4-5); and lack of bodily control (Mk. 1. 26; Lk. 4. 35).

6. FROM THE BIBLICAL MAP TO THE SPIRITUAL TERRAIN AND BEYOND

1. Stevens, José. L. *Awaken the Inner Shaman: A Guide to the Power Path of the Heart.* Sounds True, 2014; pp. 76-77.

7. DIVINATION FOR THE SAKE OF HEALING

1. Padfield, David. *The Abominations of the Canaanites.* https://padfield.com/acrobat/history/canaanite-abominations.pdf, 2009.
2. *Divination: Definition of Divination.* Merriam-Webster. https://www.merriam:webster.com/dictionary/divination.
3. Jesus' death (Mt. 16. 21, 28; 17. 22-23; 20. 17-19; Mk. 8. 31; 9. 31; 10. 32-34; Lk. 9. 22, 44; 18. 31-33; 24. 46-47; Jn. 12. 23-24, 32); the destruction of the temple and Jerusalem (Mt. 23. 37-38; 24. 2; Mk. 13. 1-2; Lk. 19. 41-44; 21. 5-6); the last days (Mt. 24. 3-44; 25. 31-46; Mk. 9. 1, 27; 13. 3-27; 14. 62; Lk. 17. 22-37; 21. 7-28; 22. 69); Peter's denial (Mt. 26. 75; Lk. 22. 61; Jn. 13. 38); Peter's death (Jn. 21. 18); the upcoming persecution of Jesus' disciples (Jn. 16. 1-4); and Judas' betrayal (Mt. 26. 24-25; Mk. 14. 16-21; Lk. 22. 21-23; Jn. 6. 70; 13. 21-30).
4. DeWaay, Bob. *The Dangers of Divination.* http://www.deceptioninthechurch.com/dangersofdivination.html.
5. Robert Fuller writes that "unchurched spirituality" is gradually reshaping the personal faith of many who belong to mainstream religious organizations. Consider, he says, the fact that 55 percent of all church members privately subscribe to some belief pertaining to the occult (e.g., astrology, reincarnation, fortune-telling, or trance channeling). Church members are also among the millions who avidly read such spiritual bestsellers as *The Road Less Traveled, The Celestine Prophecy,* and *The Seven Spiritual Laws of Success* and strive to integrate concepts from these unchurched sources into their overall worldview. Fuller, Robert C. *Spiritual, But Not Religious: Understanding Unchurched America.* Oxford University Press, 2001; p. 9.
6. The Foundation for Shamanic Studies. https://wwwshamanism.org/index.php.
7. Necromancy: https://en.wikipedia.org/wiki/Necromancy.

PART II

1. The belief that action should be based solely on reason, knowledge, and logic.
2. Virkler, Mark and Patti. *"Communion with God: Student's Study Manual."* Destiny Image Publishers, PO Box 351, Shippensburg, PA, 17257, 1983; p. 8.

8. OPENING TO MYSTERY THROUGH INTUITIVE LISTENING: TURNING ON OUR SPIRITUAL SENSES

1. Wolf, Fred Alan. *The Eagle's Quest: A Physicist's Search for Truth in the Heart of the Shamanic World.* Summit Books, 1991; pp. 193-194.
2. Wolf, Fred Alan. *The Eagle's Quest;* pp. 258-259.
3. The "third eye" is located just above and between the eyebrows. It is not a physical eye but a spiritual eye that is used to sense, see, visualize, or intuit.
4. Sheldrake, R. *Morphic Resonance and Morphic Fields—an Introduction.* https://sheldrake.org/research/morphic-resonance/introduction; pp. 7-8.

10. SHAMANIC TOOLS

1. People have been meditating for centuries. The act of meditation shifts us from a rational "beta" brain-wave (14-28 cycles/second) of sensory stimulation and goal-oriented/solution-oriented tasks to deeper levels of relaxation, indicated by alpha and theta waves, which represent a movement to a non-directed "wandering of the mind." Science Daily. *Brain Waves and Meditation.* The Norwegian University of Science and Technology, 2010. https://www.sciencedaily.com/releases/2010/03/100319210631.htm.

An Alpha state (7-14 cycles/second) is a mental state of deep relaxation and meditation. Alpha is associated with daydreams, fantasy, and denotes a state of consciousness that is detached and relaxed. Theta is a state of very deep relaxation; brain waves are slowed to a frequency of 4-7 cycles/second. People who achieve this state have access to absolute, perfect calm.

Theta brain waves can be considered the subconscious; they govern the part of our mind that lies between the conscious and the unconscious and retain memories and feelings. They direct our beliefs and our behavior and are always creative, characterized by feelings of inspiration and the spiritual.

Theta state makes one think and feel like they are on top of a mountain, totally absorbed by what's around them. A person in this state "knows" as "experience" beyond the rational intellect. They not only know "about" God but "experience" God firsthand. Being in a Theta state can be compared to a kind of trance. *Theta Healing; Theta Brain State.* https://www.thetahealing.com/about-thetahealing/thetahealing-theta-state.html.

11. SPIRITUAL POWER GIFTS

1. Take, for example, the gift of Administration. There is a Spirit-empowered gift of Administration and there is a non-Spirit, human performance of that function. In other words, a person with a natural ability to organize, find

solutions, and develop a plan can be a good administrator without the need for the Holy Spirit. This person's basis of action would be rational thought. On the other hand, the same person cannot use their same "rational" abilities to implement the power gifts of Healing, Miraculous Powers, Words of Knowledge/Wisdom, Discernment, Tongues, Prophecy, etc. The power of the Holy Spirit or helping spirits have to be drawn upon for that.

2. Additional Power Gifts:

    Faith. "The gift of faith is that unusual capacity to recognize in a given situation that which God intends to do perhaps generally and to trust him for it until he brings it to pass." Clinton, James R. *Spiritual Gifts*. Horizon House Publishers, 1985; p. 69. A gift of faith is faith beyond the capacity of normal faith. It is seeing what others cannot see, which is what S/spirit is capable of or wants to do.

    Miraculous Powers. "The supernatural ability to transform the course of natural law in such a way that divine intervention is the only possible explanation." Ford, Paul R. *Unleash Your Church: Mobilizing Spiritual Gifts Series*. Charles E. Fuller Institute, 1993; p. 159. Overall, the purpose of working miracles for a Christian was to draw people to the reality, power, and love of God.

    Tongues and the Interpretation of Tongues. "The gift of Tongues is an ability given spontaneously by the Holy Spirit to an individual to speak in a language unknown to the speaker." "The gift of the interpretation of tongues is a gift whereby a believer is given an ability spontaneously by the Holy Spirit to translate the utterances of one using the gift of tongues." Clinton, James R. *Spiritual Gifts*; p. 65.

    Exorcism. Just as everyone was given the power to heal in Mark 16, everyone also was given the power to cast out demons. But since healing is a gift, that is, some people have been given a special endowment of grace to heal, this also may apply to exorcism. In other words, some people demonstrate a special ability to deal with demonic spirits; we would call this a "gift."

3. Paul R. Ford. *"Unleash Your Church: Mobilizing Spiritual Gifts Series;"* p. 152.
4. Clinton, James R. *Spiritual Gifts;* p. 61.
5. Ford, Paul R. *Unleash Your Church*; p. 156.
6. The paralytic (Mt. 9. 2); the blind man (Jn. 9. 2-3); Zacchaeus (Lk. 19. 5); Nathanael (Jn. 1. 47-48); the woman at the well (Jn. 4. 16-18); the man at the pool of Bethesda (Jn. 5. 1-9, 14); the woman caught in adultery (Jn. 8. 1-11); and what was in people's hearts (Mt. 9. 4; Mk. 2. 8; Lk. 5. 22; 6. 8; 11. 17).
7. Ford, Paul. *Unleash Your Church*; p. 160.
8. Ford, Paul. *Unleash Your Church*; p. 157.
9. Jesus violated the Pharisees' interpretation of the Mosaic Law, not the actual law of Moses.
10. The dream is actually more extensive, more detailed. We have summarized the dream for the sake of brevity.
11. Ford, Paul. *Unleash Your Church*; p. 191.

12. ADVANCED SHAMANIC PRACTICES

1. Douglas-Klotz, N. *The Hidden Gospel: Decoding the Spiritual Message of the Aramaic Jesus*. Quest, 1999.

PART III

1. Bob is not our friend's real name. We do this to protect his anonymity.
2. We have changed our client's name to protect her anonymity.
3. There are many effective methods on the internet to show how to balance chakras.
4. Please note that some of the methods (Cognitive-Behavioral Therapy, Bio-Energetic Balancing and Massage) we use are based on our professional practices and licensures and are not to be undertaken without professional training and licensing.

YOU MAY ALSO ENJOY...

SOUL JOURNEYS

Christian Spirituality and Shamanism as Pathways for Wholeness and Understanding

Soul Journeys: Christian Spirituality and Shamanism as Pathways for Wholeness and Understanding introduces readers to Christian spirituality and Core Shamanism; and then draws on each author's knowledge and personal experiences to show readers the importance and reality of the spiritual realm in our everyday lives.

Daniel L. Prechtel is an Episcopal priest who studies and applies Core Shamanism alongside Christian prayer practices. John R. Mabry is a United Church of Christ pastor and seminary professor who uses Core Shamanism techniques in his prayer. Katrina Leathers is a Core Shamanism Practitioner and interfaith seminary dean. All three authors are spiritual directors. Together, they write about the intersection of these two great traditions, and the powerful spiritual gifts they bring.

Find it at: www.books2read.com/souljourneys